MW00915995

Freaking Idiots Guide
eBay Bundle

Contact me at

E-mail: hi@nickvulich.com

Blog: indieauthorstoolbox.com

Amazon Author Page:

- amazon.com/author/nickvulich
- amazon.com/author/nicholasvulich

Why you need to read this book

Two great bestsellers about how to sell on eBay – One Low Price!

If you've ever wanted to sell on eBay, but weren't sure how to get started these books will lead you step-by-step through the entire process.

eBay Unleashed and *Freaking Idiots Guide to Selling on eBay* are your personal guide to making money on eBay. The author, Nick Vulich, has completed over 29,000 transactions on eBay in the last thirteen years. He knows the ins and outs of selling on eBay, and is offering to walk you hand-in-hand through the selling process.

Here are just a few of the things you will learn:

1) Deciding what to sell
2) How to set up your eBay seller's account
3) How to set up your PayPal Account (so you can get paid - FAST)
4) Step-by-step instructions how to list your first item on eBay
5) Twenty-eight tips and tricks for powering up your selling
6) How to ship your items
7) How to research items so you can get the best price every time
8) An introduction to customer service - eBay style

Table of Contents

Nick Vulich

Freaking Idiots Guide to Selling on eBay

How anyone can make $100 or more everyday selling on eBay

Copyright © 2014 by Nick Vulich

Intro to New Edition

It's been just over a year now since I published the first edition of *Freaking Idiots Guide to Selling on eBay: How Anyone Can Make $100 or More Everyday Selling on eBay*. I must say I've been pleasantly surprised by the results.

The book has gone on to sell thousands of copies over the past year, and has spawned four other books about selling on eBay.

Who would have guessed?

As with anything related to eBay the pace of change is often fast and furious.

EBay releases two major seller updates every year, one in the spring and another in the fall. Last year was no exception and some of the changes made sellers jump through a number of hurdles to stay in compliance.

One of the bigger challenges had to do with picture requirements. New picture size requirements were hinted at for over a year but when they were finally released in last year's Spring Seller Update they still came as a shock to many sellers.

The key takeaway is all pictures are required to be a minimum of 500 pixels on the longest side; eBay suggests 1600 pixels for optimum quality. Another section of the new picture requirements limits watermarks and other text sellers superimpose over pictures.

Not long after the new policy went into effect sellers found their listings being taken down for picture violations whenever they featured gallery photos showing product logos. eBay's automated system assumed the logos were text superimposed over the picture and took the listings down. The work around for most sellers is to be sure you don't feature any logos in your gallery pictures. Instead lead with a picture of your item, and then show pictures of the tags.

The 2013 Spring Seller Update included major changes regarding eBay stores and seller fees.

For the first time eBay tied listing prices to store levels offering a number of free listings each month depending upon which store level sellers have. Under the new arrangement casual sellers continue to receive 50 free listing each month. After that they are charged thirty cents for each additional auction or fixed price listing. Final value fees are ten percent. Basic Store sellers receive 150 free listings every month, and pay 25 cents for each additional auction style listing, 20 cents for each additional fixed price listing and from 4% to 9% final value fees. Premium Store sellers receive 500 free listings per month, and pay 15 cents for each additional auction style listing and 10 cents for each additional fixed price listing and from 4% to 9% final value fees. Anchor Store sellers receive 2500 free listings per month, and pay 10 cents for each additional auction listing and five cents for each additional fixed price listing and from 4% to 9% final value fees.

The Fall Seller Update was less traumatic for sellers. The biggest change involved eBay's Hassle Free Return Policy. Sellers were encouraged to opt in as a way to increase their customer service and sales. Some of the benefits allow sellers to select the individual items they want to include, the ability to totally automate returns, the ability to offer product replacements in lieu of returns, and a guarantee that return shipping will never cost more than your original shipping costs (if you use eBay shipping labels).

The Fall 2013 Seller Update made changes to eBay's me pages; they're now called eBay profiles. The look is reminiscent of Facebook. You have a large banner, and a smaller profile picture. Interested visitors can check out your profile picture by clicking on your seller id.

When buyers click on your profile they see your pictures, a short tagline about your business, your feedback profile, and five items you have for sale.

After this they see a new area recently developed by eBay called Collections. Collections is a Pinterest like feature where buyers and sellers can highlight eBay items they are following. Very few people are currently using Collections, but you can expect that to change as we move into the New Year. The major problem I see here is a lot of the items on eBay don't lend themselves to being displayed this way.

As you move further down the page you see a list of people following your profile, and then a list of your top three eBay reviews and Guides. My thought is because of the space eBay is devoting to them eBay Reviews and guides will become even more important to driving sales. See my book *eBay Subject Matter Expert: 5 Weeks to Becoming an eBay Subject Matter Expert.*

Another inclusion in every seller update centers on category changes and updates. Many times eBay changes category specifics adding drop down menus for size, color, style, manufacturer, etc.

While the 2014 Seller Updates have not been released yet many sellers are speculating there will be a number of mandatory opt ins. Two of the programs eBay has been pushing heavily are their Global Shipping Program and Managed Returns. At the present time both policies are optional, but rumor has it by the end of 2014 all sellers will be forced to enroll in them.

Time will tell if this is true or not.

Cassini search is another factor causing grief for eBay sellers.

Many sellers have discovered Cassini search doesn't play well with listings that have HTML code in them, especially when it is at the top of the listing. What a lot of sellers have noted is their listings either don't come up in search at all, or else they come up at the bottom of search. When they strip out the HTML code, especially listing headers, they immediately rank higher in search.

My suggestion to you is if you are one of the seller's whose listing are consistently lagging in sales, or if when you search for your listings you can't find them, you need to rethink your listing strategy.

If you have a large number of listings on eBay start with fifty or a hundred of them. Strip the listing header out of some of them, and strip all of the HTML code out of another group. Give it a couple of days then verify what it does for your listing visibility and sales. This way you can see how your eBay listings are impacted by having HTML code in them.

HTML code in your listings has also been found to negatively impact your visibility in mobile search.

Why is this important? Because right now mobile sales account for nearly one-third of all ecommerce sales and over the next year that number is expected to move closer to fifty percent. If your listings aren't showing in mobile search you're losing nearly fifty percent of your potential sales.

I tested listing visibility myself by searching for and displaying over fifty of my eBay listings using my Android phone. Ten of the listings didn't come up at all when I searched for them; the remainder of them displayed so-so on my Android phone.

The big problem I experienced was viewing listings that included embedded pictures. They pulled up ok; I could scroll through the listings fine; but I couldn't enlarge the pictures. Compared to listings that used eBay's picture hosting service, listings with embedded pictures are at a huge disadvantage when viewed on mobile. Pictures that use eBay's photo service – display full screen on a phone or tablet. If there is more than one picture you can scroll through all of them by toggling the arrow that displays on the pictures. Embedded pictures remain their same wimpy size. Try it yourself, and decide which one you think would sell best.

My suggestion is to take a close look at your listings and ensure they are optimized for mobile.

I think too often we concentrate on wanting to make our listings look awesome. I know when I was initially growing my sales a fancy template was at the top of my A-List and I invested thousands of dollars developing and tweaking it. In today's eBay marketplace you need to reevaluate this strategy, and really test to see what maximizes your sales.

I love a good template and a fancy store, but they don't pay the bill if the sales don't follow.

Product Sourcing

Product sourcing is another subject I didn't discuss much in the first edition of this book.

Where I did talk about it was when I explained to sellers how easy it is to find items you can sell around the house. My thought was to take baby steps and start with things you already have. I still think that's a good strategy to begin with. There's no sense jumping head-over-heels into something before you know if it's going to work for you or not.

After you have ten or twenty sales under your belt you can start thinking about what comes next.

When I first started selling online Yahoo and eBay were the two big online auction players. I bought baseball card "lots" on Yahoo and resold them on eBay. A few years later when Yahoo shut down their auctions I started buying most of my inventory on eBay and reselling it there too. It's an awesome strategy that still works for me. I rarely have to look anywhere else for new inventory.

The reason it works so well for me is most people don't see the real value in what they have.

I sell old magazine articles and prints. Most of my inventory comes from bound volumes sellers post on eBay for $5.00 to $25.00 each. When I buy a bound volume, I can break it down into anywhere from twenty to fifty articles and prints that I can resell for anywhere from $15.00 to $50.00 each. Not a bad profit.

Of course there are other costs. I have to buy holders for each separate article, and I need to pay twenty to fifty individual listing fees of ten cents each and every month. The result is my inventory is incredibly cheap, but my eBay fees can easily eat up one third or more of my income.

It's a give and take situation that I've found works well for me.

Another thing that works for me is to keep an eye on eBay for poorly listed items. A lot of sellers don't put enough thought into their listings. I've seen sellers list the first and second issues of Sports Illustrated Magazine from 1954 and 1955 without mentioning the baseball card inserts or showing pictures of them. When I spot these auctions I normally send a quick email to the seller verifying the cards are present and intact and if they are I pounce on the item.

You can find similar situations with clothes, books, sports cards, whatever it is that interests you. My suggestion is to spend a half hour to an hour every week scouring listings for similar opportunities.

The next best place to find inventory is your local Walmart, Target, TJ Maxx, or just about any retailer. Retail stores manage their inventory on a close time line. They receive seasonal items, offer them at full price for the first few weeks, and by the time they are midway through the season they start marking prices down. As they inch closer to the end of the season they're anxious to remove any leftover inventory so they dramatically slash prices – sometimes by 75 percent or more.

Smart sellers keep an eye out for these opportunities and buy everything they can get their hands on. Some sellers shoot them back up on eBay right away, but profit minded sellers sock seasonal items away and hold onto them until the start of the season next year. That way they can sell last year's closeouts at full price or close to it going into the new year.

If you can scrape up a few extra bucks, or if you have some extra room on your credit cards give it a shot. Again, don't blow the bank hoping to make one big score. Baby step it the first time or two to make sure the system will work for you.

If you buy your groceries at Walmart every week spend some time in the clearance aisles. Take a few notes about what you find. Check what those items are selling for on eBay when you get home. Or if you're really eager to get started check the going price on your cell phone while you're still in the clearance aisle.

For sellers who use this method a lot I'd recommend *Barcode Booty: How I found and sold $2 million of 'junk' on eBay and Amazon, And you can, too, using your phone* by Steve Weber. It will open up a whole new world of sourcing and selling opportunities for you.

Thrift stores like the Salvation Army, Good Will, and the DAV Store are another great source of inventory. These stores receive new inventory daily, and you never know what's going to turn up there. Clothing sellers make a killing shopping at these stores, because they can find a good selection of brand name, gently used, and new clothes here. Other items you can find are books, DVD's, jewelry, and collectibles. Regular shoppers at thrift stores take note of which days they change prices, run special promos, and keep an eye out for coupons where they can save an additional fifty percent on many of their purchases.

If you source a lot of your inventory at thrift stores, yard sales, and resale shops I would recommend the book *9 Easy Ways to Start Making Money on eBay in 72 Hours or Less* by Michelle Angell. It's an excellent primer for new eBay sellers.

Yard sales, estate sales, and local auctions are another smart way to acquire inventory. Similar to shopping at thrift stores, you never know what you're going to come across. My suggestion is to make some small purchases first and test the waters. Use your cell phone to research items before making bigger purchases. Some sellers have one person work the sale, and another at home by the computer checking prices as they call or text them.

Other sellers list items for neighbors, friends, and relatives. They take a cut of the selling price after fees, and pick up additional customers through referrals.

You can choose one of these methods, or a combination of them. The main thing is to find a system that works for you.

Old Introduction

Are you wondering how you can make a few hundred bucks fast, without hitting the streets? Would you like to know how you can put $100 in your hands, whenever you're running a little short on funds? Would you like to have your own personal money machine?

This book can help you with all of these things.

What you are about to learn is how to make $100 everyday selling on eBay.

Unlike many other books you may have read, this book is going to be short, and to the point. After all, you're anxious to put everything in motion, so we're going to take several short, simple, baby steps to move you in the right direction.

What I'm going to give you is a plan you can follow over and over again, to make money now – and in the future, whenever you find yourself strapped for a little cash.

First let me tell you what this isn't. It's not a get rich quick scheme, where you can put in fifteen minutes, and have $1000 in your mailbox the next morning. It's more like a job, with lots of overtime, and hard work. But, if you follow the plan –

I can promise that you will have an extra $100 in your pocket whenever you need it ...

Why Listen to Me

H ey there, Nick Vulich here.

If you're like me, I'm sure you're probably a little skeptical about taking advice from someone without knowing a little bit about them first.

I've been selling on eBay since 1999. Most of my online customers know me as history-bytes, although I've also operated as its old news, back door video, and sports card one.

I've sold 30,004 items for a total of $411,755.44 over the past fifteen years, and that's just on my history-bytes id. Right now I've cut way back on eBay selling to focus on my writing, but I still keep my hat in the game. That way I can stay current with the challenges my readers face every day when they go to sell on eBay.

I've been an eBay Power Seller or Top Rated Seller for most of the past fifteen years, which means I've met eBay's sales and customer satisfaction goals.

Right off, that tells you I'm not coming at you out of left field, with all sorts of half-baked ideas I dreamed up after reading a half-dozen eBay how-to books. Most of the tips I'm going to share with you, I learned from the school of hard-knocks. I learned them from being out there selling every day, experimenting with new products, and new listing methods.

I've written about selling on eBay. The first two, *Freaking Idiots Guide to Selling on eBay*, and *eBay Unleashed*, are aimed more towards how to get started selling on eBay. *eBay 2014* is directed at more advanced sellers and tackles many of the challenges top rated sellers face in the eBay marketplace. *eBay Subject Matter Expert* suggests a different approach to selling on eBay – building a platform where customers recognize you as an expert in your niche, and buy from you because of your knowledge in that field. *Sell It Online* gives a brief overview of selling on eBay, Amazon, Etsy, and Fiver. *How to Make Money Selling Old Books & Magazines on eBay* talks specifically about what I know best, how to sell books and magazines on eBay.

Taken together these books give you all the information you need to succeed on eBay. My goal is to help you become as successful as you wish to be.

Let's get started…

Getting Started

e **Bay Account.** The first thing you're going to need is an eBay account.

The good news is – They're free, and you can sign up for one in less than five minutes. If you don't already have an eBay account you can sign up for one now by visiting *get started with eBay*.

When you sign up you're going to ask for some simple information. eBay will ask for your name and email address. Next you will be asked to supply a user name. This is how people will come to know you on eBay, so be sure to put some thought into it. If you know what you want to sell, it will make it easier.

I sell historical paper and ephemera, so my eBay moniker is history-bytes. It's short, simple, and says something about what I sell.

If you want to sell trains and your name is Dan, you could try danstrains.

If your name is Mona, and your reason for selling on eBay is to get some cash for Christmas presents, you could try: monaschristmascash.

If you can't come up with a good idea right now, don't sweat it. eBay lets you change your id every 30 days.

PayPal account. You're also going to need a way to get paid. PayPal is the simplest and most popular payment method on eBay. If you don't have a PayPal account, you can get one by visiting *sign up for PayPal.*

When you sign up you will be asked if you want a personal account or a business account. The choice is entirely up to you. If you go with the personal account, and later decide eBay selling is really your thing, you can upgrade to a business account then.

The really great thing about PayPal is, as soon as your customer pays them, PayPal pays you. One option I would recommend is a PayPal debit card. With it you have access to your money immediately. Transferring money to your bank account can take 3 to 5 days.

eBay also allows several other payment methods.

Buyers are allowed to pay by snail mail sending, you a check or money order. However, sellers are not allowed to say they will accept checks or money orders in their item listings. If a buyer asks if they can send cash, check, or money order – it is ok for you to let them.

Sellers can also accept Propay, Skrill, Paymate, and credit card processing through your own merchant service provider. If you offer local pickup for your items, sellers are allowed to pay when they pick up their item.

A few other things that will make your eBay experience run smoother are a digital camera or scanner depending upon the type of item you are selling. Your cell phone camera will also work just fine.

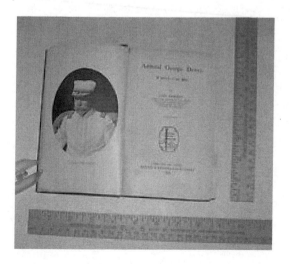

A ruler will also come in handy. Don't worry. We're not going to take any complicated measurements or anything. What the ruler does is add a scale for someone to help them picture the size of your item. In these days of close-up photography it's often hard to imagine how big something is. A ruler with large numbers makes it easy for buyers to understand the dimensions of the item they are buying. You can say six inches, but a picture often says it better. It's easier to visualize something if you can see it.

I've seen other sellers do this with a hundred dollar bill. Everyone is familiar with money. Set your item down by a hundred dollar bill and people instantly make the connection about its size.

Finally before you get started find a nice quiet spot where you can work without interruptions.

What Should You Sell

O ne of the hardest things for most people is figuring out what they want to sell on eBay.

It doesn't have to be that hard. Most people get started on eBay by selling items they have around the house. Look around you. You probably have a lot of great things scattered all over the house that you're no longer using.

Do you have some shoes you don't wear anymore? Have you upgraded your old cell phone in the past year? If you have kids did they outgrow any of their clothes? Remember that ugly sweater mom gave you for Christmas last year? Has anyone taken any college classes recently? Someone is going to need those textbooks.

We bought everyone Kindle Fire's last year after Christmas, but one of the kids decided she couldn't live without an iPad, and now that Kindle just sits there unused. Bet it could fetch a couple of bucks on eBay?

Do you get the idea? We all have things we no longer use sitting around the house. They're still great items. And chances are pretty good, there's somebody out there who'd be willing to pay you a few bucks to get them.

The reason most people don't get past this first step is because they have a hard time putting a value on the things around them. Sure you no longer use a land line phone, but chances are someone else will. You can drop the phone in the trash can, take it to Good Will – or you can take a long hard look at it and see that phone for what it is - twenty-five bucks towards the hundred dollars you need.

Notice how putting a dollar value on something can make it more attractive?

Let's take another walk around the house with our "money vision" goggles on. What other great items did you miss the first time around?

Take a close look at your stamp collection. Do you collect baseball cards, Hummel figurines, or beer cans? Do you have any duplicates? Are there any items that no longer fit in with your collection? Often times, collections evolve over time, and you find yourself with a number of pieces that no longer really fit in with your current collection. People often upgrade their stamps and baseball cards over time as they find better copies. You start off with a filler card, and when you can afford it you swap it out for a better card. The good news is – you're not the only one who does this. Lots of other collectors do the same thing. That bumpy edged, creased Hank Aaron card may be just what they're looking for to complete a 1955 Topps set.

Does anyone in your house play video games? Most homes today have three or four video games systems, many of which are no longer used. Take a few minutes to look for games you haven't played in a while. Chances are someone on eBay is looking for those games, or game systems.

My dad had this habit of stashing all of our old toys, comic books, and such in the rafters of the garage. If I remember correctly we had Match Box cars, baseball cards, G I

Joes, Rock Em Sock Em Robots, and lots of other cool stuff. Might be worth a trip to visit the parents, don't you think?

A quick glance at eBay shows Rock Em Sock Em Robots in good condition (with the original box) selling for $187.25, with 13 bids, and 14 hours to go. Somebody's going to have a nice payday!

Now I know there are going to be a few sour pusses out there who say they "got nothing." Like Charlie Brown at Halloween, they've got a bag full of rocks.

Suppose there really is nothing in your house you can sell. How are you going to get that $100 you need?

Many times it can be as easy as going to the store. Several Christmases ago my wife was shopping at Jo Ann Fabrics and came across Bedazzler's discounted to five bucks. She had been looking at them on eBay, and they were selling for $80 to $100 each, so when she got home the first thing she did was check eBay again. Still $80 to $100. She compared her Bedazzler to those selling on eBay, and sure enough – they were the same. Those eBay sellers didn't have any "magic Bedazzler's." They were just getting a whole lot more money for the ones they had.

To make a long story short, we bought every Bedazzler Jo Ann Fabric's had, as well as all of the ones available from every JoAnn's within fifty miles.

I sold 87 Bedazzler's for $50 to $75 over a six week period. I probably could have gotten more money for them, but I unloaded them too quickly and flooded the market.

I like old books. Occasionally I will visit used bookstores looking for new items I can sell. Last summer I discovered three county history books from the late 1800's. I got them for $100 to $125 each. Within two weeks, I sold them all on eBay for $250 to $400 each.

If you go to estate sales they have loads of great stuff waiting for you to discover. Local auctions offer the same opportunity. Remember to put your "money vision" goggles on when you visit these places. You will be amazed by all of the profitable things you've been walking by for your entire life.

As you see it doesn't take a lot of time or effort to find items to sell. You just need to adjust the way you look at the things around you. Profitable items are everywhere once you open your eyes to them.

Now that you have a better idea of the types of things you can sell, the next section is going to go into the nitty-gritty of how to sell them. This is important to you because eBay has millions of sellers, and they are all competing with you to get the buyers attention.

Luckily for you, most sellers have no idea what they have, or how to sell it.

eBay Selling 101

L et me repeat what I said in the last chapter.

Most sellers have no idea what they have, or how to sell it ...

What's the secret to selling your item for the most money possible?

It's easy...

Put yourself in your buyer's shoes. Take a minute to think about why a buyer would want what you're selling. Ask yourself who is the ideal customer for it? Why would anyone want your old Kindle? What can they do with it? What could they do with it? Most people never think of using it for more than reading. Did you?

My suggestion is to think of all of the ways an item can be used, and pick out five or six of them to sell your buyer on.

In the case of the Kindle, obviously you can use it to read e-books. Most sellers are going to leave it at that. It's easy. They don't have to put a whole lot of thought into it. Shoot a picture. Say I've got a Kindle Fire. Give me a hundred bucks.

Unfortunately, if you do the same thing, your poor Kindle Fire is going to be lost in the crowd. A quick search shows 1208 of them on sale today.

If you really want to sell your item you've got to put a little pizazz in your description. What if we said our Kindle was a great internet tablet for people on the go? And, now that I think about it, my youngest daughter is always downloading movies and TV shows to watch on it. It's great for email, and oh yeah! With a USB cord, you can move your documents over to your Kindle. And, did I mention, you can also download music, and listen to it with your ear-buds.

It doesn't really matter what you're selling. You need to think outside of the box when you're listing items on eBay.

I specialize in old books and magazines. Every day old volumes of Harper's Magazine from the 1850's to the early 1900's come up for sale on eBay. They consistently sell for $10 to $15 each. The majority of sellers pop up a picture of the dilapidated old leather cover falling apart from age, and say it's an old book in poor condition. Very few of them open the book to look at all the great woodcut illustrations. Why not show a few of these? Perhaps it would help to list some of the contents? It will take some extra time, but the odds are any time you spend attending to these details will mean the difference between selling your book for $10 or for $50.

Let me give you an example.

There's a book seller I've been following on eBay for five or six years now. He sells the same books everyone else sells does. The only difference is he receives dozens of bids on his books, and often sells them for $100 to $200. His competitors who don't put as much work into their listings regularly receive $15 to $25 for the same books.

Any guesses why he receives so much more money for his books? He puts in the extra time to craft a great description. He tells people what the book is about. He shares passages from it. And, he isn't stingy with pictures. Many of his listings have twenty or more pictures in them. Sure, you can say a book has great illustrations. A few well-chosen pictures will show buyers how great those illustrations are.

With all that being said, what's the perfect description?

What I suggest is that you write the best description you can for each item. Don't worry about how long it takes. Concentrate on telling potential buyers everything they need to know to make an informed decision.

Let's Start Selling

The first thing you need to know is selling on eBay isn't free. It's going to cost you a little money. The nice thing about eBay is casual sellers don't have to pay any fees up front. Normally eBay bill you about thirty days after you complete the sale. This gives you plenty of time to sell your item, and collect your payment, before you pay eBay.

As an eBay member without an eBay Store, eBay gives you an extra bonus for selling.

Your first fifty auction or fixed price listings are FREE. You only pay final value fees if your item sells.

Used properly, and combined with your great items, this should be more than enough opportunities to make some extra cash.

About eBay fees. Depending upon what you are selling, eBay is going to charge you a 4% to 10% final value fee when your item sells. It's a cost of doing business. Consider it your rent. If you have a store, you have to pay the landlord. If you list your stuff in the paper you have to pay for the ad. If you sell at a flea market you have to pay for your booth. eBay is no different. You have to pay to play.

eBay is the place where everybody gathers to checkout, and buy, other people's junk. If you're not there, you're not going to make the hundred bucks you need.

Different Ways to Sell

If you're not familiar with eBay, there are several different ways to list your items for sale. The three main types of listings are: 1) Auction, 2) Fixed Price, and 3) Classified Listings.

Of the three, auction and fixed price are what you will be using most.

Auction listings allow potential buyers to bid against each other for your item, much as they would when attending a local auction. The way it works is – bidders place what is called a "proxy bid." When they do this they tell eBay they are willing to spend up to a certain amount, $10.00, $15.00, whatever they set as their upper bid limit. From here eBay places your bid for you up to your maximum bid. If the seller starts her auction at $9.99, and your "proxy bid" is $25.00, eBay will place your bid for $9.99, the seller's minimum acceptable bid. If someone else places a bid, they will advance yours, up to your $25.00 limit.

Fixed price listings are much like walking into your local Wal-Mart or Best Buy. You see a price on the shelf, and that is the price you have to pay. There is no bargaining, finagling, or whatever. Whoever agrees to pay the asking price gets the item.

Classified Listings are more informational. They are a way for businesses to get information out there about what they are doing. An example would be someone selling eBay training seminars. They can give information about their training seminars, and give you an email address or phone number to follow up with for more information (something not allowed in auction or fixed price listings).

eBay also offers variations on the above listings that everyone should consider using. The most important of these tools is **Buy-It-Now**. By adding buy-it-now to your auction listing you have the ability to start your item at a low price, yet reach for the sky. If someone exercises the buy-it-now option, the auction ends, and the bidder wins the item. If on the other hand, someone makes the minimum bid, the buy-it-now option disappears, and the only way to buy the item is by bidding on it.

The way I use buy-it-now is to set my starting price at the lowest price I am willing to accept. Then I set my buy-it-now price at three or four times my starting price. It's the price I would ideally like to receive.

Best offer is another spin eBay offers for fixed price auctions. Best offer is just like it sounds. You price the item, and potential buyers can buy your item at the fixed price, or they can send you an offer. Be prepared to laugh a little, and cry a little, at some of the offers you are going to receive. I had one guy make a $1.00 offer on fifty different items I was selling at $25.00 each. You would think he'd have better things to do than waste both of our time making low ball offers.

What I've found is the majority of people will offer you between one-half and two-thirds of your asking price. Some of buyers will low-ball you with a string of $5.00 offers; others are happy to save a few bucks to help them cover shipping costs.

The good news is eBay lets you totally automate the process. When you set up the best offer option you can tell eBay to accept all offers over such and such a price, and to automatically decline all offers below a certain amount. This way you don't have to deal with any of these low-ball offers. The only offers eBay will send you are the ones that come in between your decline price and your accept price, so you can manually decide whether to accept them or not.

For example, if I set my accept price at $17.00, and my decline price at $10.00, eBay will accept all offers I receive over $17.00. If an offer comes in under $10.00, they don't bother me with it. It someone makes an offer between $10.00 and $17.00, they send a message to the person making an offer to tell them the seller "is considering their offer." Then it's up to me. I can accept their offer. I can send a counter offer ("Hey - $10.00 is too low, but I would take $15.00"). Then we can bargain back and forth like this for another three tries.

Your First Listing

This section is going to cover everything you need to know to make your first sale on eBay. When you are done you will know how to write a compelling title that will bring hundreds of potential buyers to your listing, how to write a description that will leave them drooling for more, and how to shoot pictures that sell.

To get started selling you click **sell** at the top of the eBay page, or visit the Tell us what you want to sell page.

If your item has a UPC or ISBN enter it when you are prompted. If it doesn't have either of these or if you have a unique item select browse categories. This will let you choose a category to list your item in. If you have an older book without an ISBN, select fiction or non-fiction, then drill down into the category that best describes your book. If you're selling a woman's leather jacket, select *women's clothing >> coats and jackets.*

Write a Compelling Title

eBay gives you 88 characters to describe your item. The more information you put into it, the more people are going to see your item.

Why? Because different things are important to different people. Some people search for iPod; others search for iPod 8 GB; others are more interested in "certified;" still others for "Apple certified." If you want to buy on the cheap, but still get something good, you may want "refurbished."

Let's look at a few titles currently listed on eBay for the iPod Touch…

.Apple iPod Touch 4th Generation Black 8GB (Used)

.Apple iPod Touch 32 GB Black (4th Generation) Apple Certified Refurbished

.Great Condition!!! No reserve. Apple iPod Touch 4th Generation Black 32 GB

.Apple iPod Touch 4th Generation 8GB –MC55OLL- works great-camera-earphone

.Apple iPod Touch 4th Generation 16GB New in Factory Sealed Box

Let's take a closer look at those titles. The one thing that stands out about all of them is they are all loaded with keyword rich details.

. 8GB, 16 GB, 32 GB

. black / white

. 3rd generation / 4th generation

. Apple iPod Touch

. IPod touch

. factory sealed in box

. Apple Certified Refurbished

. camera

. earphone

Are you starting to get the idea?

Yeah! It's an iPod, but that's only one small piece of the puzzle. It's all in the details. What people really want is an iPod Touch with one or all of the above features. If you're title doesn't include the keywords a buyer is looking for, he is going to move on to the next listing.

When you write a title its sole purpose is to get potential buyers to stop, click into your auction, and take a closer look at your pictures and description.

Let's look at another item

If you type "Nike men's shoes" in the eBay search box, there are 219,158 pairs listed. That's like getting caught in rush hour traffic on the Eisenhower. Your shoes aren't going anywhere.

Without more details your poor shoes are going to be lost in the rush.

What we need to do is level the playing field. You have to think about what's important to people when they're looking for a new pair of shoes.

Some of the things they're going to look for are:

. size

. color

. style (athletic, loafer, dress, work boot)

. width (d, ee)

. model number

. new / used

. new in box

. easy returns

. men's / women's / children's

If you want to sell those shoes, you need to fit as many of these keywords as you can in the 88 characters eBay allows you for a title. If you miss just one, you will reduce your chances of making a sale.

A search on the following keywords (men's Nikes 10 ee new in box) reduced the number of pairs shown from 219,158 to six.

Obviously you have a better chance of selling those shoes when you're one of six pairs, rather than one of several hundred thousand.

Remember your title doesn't have to be a complete sentence. It doesn't even have to make sense when you read it. It just needs to have enough keywords in it, so potential buyers can easily find your item.

The takeaway here is to laser focus your title. If you're unsure what keywords should be in your title, search eBay to see which keywords other sellers are using in their listings. You can also search the manufacturers selling page for keyword ideas.

Picture It Sold

You've heard the saying "a picture is worth a thousand words." On eBay a picture can often times be worth a thousand dollars.

You can have the best title, a great description, and a killer price, but if your pictures suck you're not likely to make a deal.

When people are ready to buy something, especially expensive items, they demand great pictures. The best example of this is your local car dealer. They don't stop with one picture. More often than not you will find twenty to twenty-five pictures for every car they are selling. Your car dealer knows most customers shop on the internet before they come into the dealership to make a purchase.

As a result car dealers give you a virtual tour of the car with the pictures they take. On the outside, they show you front, back, and both sides. There is at least one picture of the engine, a view into the trunk, the upper dash board, the odometer showing the mileage, the floor – front and back, and close ups of any damage.

You can learn a lot about the type of pictures you need to include in your eBay listings by studying car dealer listings. The lighting is always perfect. Every picture is perfectly centered. Smart car dealers never use a bad picture. They know one bad picture can kill the entire deal.

Plan your pictures the same way. Include at least one overall view of your item. You want close up detailed pictures of

there is damage – don't just say it in the
ke sure to include one or two pictures of the
Let potential buyers decide for themselves how
e is.

eBay lets you upload 12 free pictures with every listing.
Include as many as you need to tell your story.

Beginning in January 2013, eBay is requiring all photos to
be a least 500 pixels on the longest end. They suggest 1600 pixels
for the best results. I size my pictures at 1000 pixels on the
longest end. Experiment with different picture sizes to decide
which ones work best for you.

How do you resize your pictures?

If you are only running a few auctions you can manually
resize them using Paint. To do this import your pictures into
Paint, select the resize tool, and resave them. In my case I
normally scan 150 to 200 pictures a day. Resizing that many
pictures manually would be a major time suck. I automate the
process with Adobe Light Room. Using Light Room I can
import all of my pictures with the click of a button, optimize
them with two or three mouse clicks, and export them back to
my desktop - all in less than five minutes.

The key takeaway here is to get as many pictures as you
need to sell your item. If the lighting is off or the picture is off
center retake it. A few extra minutes invested in redoing a poor
picture will pay off when you make the sale.

Crafting a Great Description

Think of your item description as your sales pitch. The more useful information you share about your item, the better your chances of selling it at a premium price. Expand on all of those keywords you included in the title. Take your time to craft a compelling story that convinces potential buyers how much they need your item.

First and foremost be honest.

When you're writing about all of the great features your item has be sure to mention any defects it has. The last thing you want to do is make a sale, and have it blow up in your face, because of a scratch, or any other minor defect. The truth is most people aren't worried about minor flaws or defects as long as they know about them when they are making the purchase. What bothers people is finding out about any problems after they've laid down their hard earned money.

What makes a great description?

Let's look at a few, and you will get a better idea of how you can craft a winning description every time.

Up for auction is a rare U.S. Senate document of Dubuque, Iowa historical interest, a March 30, 1846 report, 26 pages long, detailing the findings of the Committee on Private Land Claims regarding the claims of Julien Dubuque and August Chouteau and their heirs to "a tract of one hundred and forty-eight thousand... arpens of land, situate on the river Mississippi, at a place called the Spanish Mines, about four hundred and forty miles from St. Louis." After the Louisiana Purchase, the U.S. government had to determine the validity of various French and Spanish land claims. In the document, the history of Dubuque and Chouteau's claim to the land, including their purchase of the land from the "Sac and Fox nation of Indians" in 1788. Detailed discussion within about the validity of the claim, about the validity of the sale by the tribes, and much more. Today, this area contains the city of Dubuque, Iowa. A fascinating document. Originally bound into a larger bound volume of Senate reports, but discovered as such, and in total, a self-contained work of its own. Binding still holding. Quite rare. Good luck

---

This auction is for a like new condition Field Gear thick supple leather with super soft Genuine Raccoon Tail. Zip, removable hood. Jacket parka tag size missing but fits like a man's large or extra-large, please see measurements to determine best fit. This jacket is great, with no flaws and looks barely worn! This jacket would make a great gift, or wear it yourself and impress your friends and family. Get this jacket in time for the upcoming fall and winter to look good and stay warm! Make this yours now, and please check out my store.

Measures shoulder to shoulder 21 inches, pit to pit 25 inches, top of shoulder to bottom 33 inches, top of cuff to top of shoulder 24 inches.

It is that time of year again. Winter time. We are now starting to bring out our high end winter clothing. We have over

300 pieces of Northface, Spyder, Pendleton, Patagonia an(of other high end clothing. Be sure to keep on checking b because we will be putting up a lot of things in the next three months. I also have a lot of winter boots available.

Up for sale is a men's Columbia heavy duty jacket in size XL. Great anorak pull over jacket. Full side zipper. Super good looking and warm. If you know quality, then you know Columbia is the finest clothing out there. This is the same brand that my family wears. Super high end and expensive. You will look fantastic in this clothing. It will keep you warm and dry.

_____

Are you beginning to see a pattern?

Each seller is telling a story, and building value into their items. The first one on the document tells you in a short concise description what you can expect to find in it, why it is important, and what condition it is in.

The two listings for clothing build on emotion. "This is same brand my family wears." "Impress your friends and family." "You will look fantastic in this clothing."

The first clothing item also gives you exact measurements. That way there is no guessing. Anyone who orders can be sure the coat will fit them. The end result is buyers will be less likely to return their purchases.

Another takeaway from the last item is the pitch to look at the seller's other items. "Be sure to keep checking back...I also have a lot of winter boots available."

When you start writing your descriptions refer back to these listings. You want to include specific details about the item you are selling – size, color, brand, and any defects. If you can - appeal to any emotions, "look great," "feel good," "be the envy of your friends and neighbors." People are drawn to items they like, but any car salesman can tell you – emotion closes more sales, than anything else.

Finally if you are selling complimentary products, such as jackets and pants, or a series of books or movies – be sure to suggest that buyers check out your other auctions.

Price Your Items to Sell

Congratulations. You've done it.

You've written a killer title loaded with keywords. Your description has left them drooling over your item. It tells everything a buyer needs to know to make an informed decision, and it appeals to their emotions

Now all you've got to do is price it right.

More sales are lost at this step, than anywhere else in the sales process. Too often sellers are overly attached to their items. Especially if it is an item they've owned since childhood, or one with a family history.

You see it on every episode of Pawn Stars. Rick or Cory call in an expert to appraise an item, and the expert appraises it at $1000. Yet the owner stubbornly holds on to their idea of what the item is worth. Because the item is old, or has sentimental value, or they have so much money invested in it they feel they need to get a certain price, often times $500 or $1000 more than the expert appraised it at.

Bad idea! **An item is only worth what someone is willing to pay for it.**

Sometimes this fact works in your favor, other times you have to shrug your shoulders, and take what you can get.

In my case, I sell old magazine articles that have no set value. There is no official price so I've learned to wing it, and set my prices by experimenting with where they sell best. I know from past experience what topics are going to sell for more money, or sell quicker. On those items, I jump my price twenty or thirty dollars, and many times I get it. If the item doesn't sell in a reasonable time I drop the price and take what I can get for it.

A lot of items don't allow you this luxury. They sell day in and day out in a very narrow price range, and if you jump out of that price range – No sale.

Here's one of the best ways to set your price to assure a quick sell through, especially if you are a new seller.

Do a completed item search on eBay using the advanced search feature.

To do a completed item search, find the search box at the top of the eBay page. To the right of the words **SEARCH** it will say **ADVANCED**. Click on **ADVANCED**, and it will take you to another set of search options.

Enter the keywords you want to search on. You can choose to search in just one category, or search listings in all categories (I would recommend this one). A little further down where it says **search including** be sure to check off by **completed listings**. As you scroll down you will see there are a lot more options you can search by. Unless you are looking for some really specialized information the only other two selections I would consider are Auction and Buy It Now under the Selling Formats category.

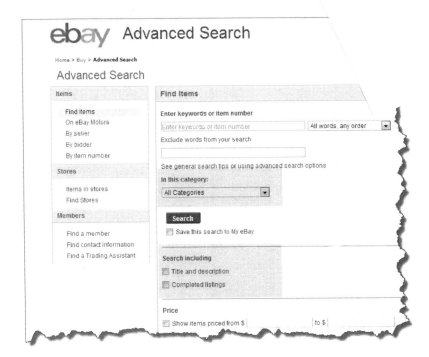

A quick look through completed listings for the last week or two will give you a good idea of the price range your item has sold in. You can drill down even more by clicking on the listings that sold for the most money and garnered the most bids.

Take a close look at the keywords the seller used in the title; what they said in the description; the type and number of pictures they included; and finally look at what price the seller started the listing at. No use reinventing the wheel, write all of this down and include as much of it as you can in your own listings.

The biggest advantage of using completed item search is you can see exactly what items like yours have sold for. If enough items have sold you will have a very good idea how much money your item should sell for, and what price you should start your listing at.

There are several pricing theories you may want to consider.

One school of thought holds that you should price every item at 99 cents and let the market set the price. This works well with items that sell in large quantities and normally sell within a tight price range. Electronics are a good example where this strategy can work for you. There are always plenty of buyers ready to pounce on an iPad, iPhone, or laptop. Starting your item at 1 cent or 99 cents is normally going to spark a bidding war and bring you the best possible price.

Other people prefer to know their item is going to bring at least a certain price. If you're selling an item that normally brings $100 to $125, you can price it at $85, and add a Buy-It-Now option for $125. This guarantees a minimum price if your item sells, and gives you a shot at getting a better price if someone exercises your Buy-It-Now.

Whatever you do, think really hard on using the 99 cent strategy if you're selling a collectible or one of a kind item. Often times a collectible, no matter how rare, only has one buyer at any given time. If you can't spark a bidding war that $100 or $500 item could end up selling for 99 cents.

Talk about bringing out the Christmas Scrooge. That would give you the bah hum-bugs for quite some time to come.

Ship Like a Pro

The biggest thing to keep in mind about shipping is that you are responsible for the item until the seller receives it.

If it gets lost in the mail, you need to make good on it. If it arrives damaged, you need to make good on it. If your shipment arrives incomplete, and the buyer says all the pieces aren't there, you need to make good on it.

You need to package your item properly. If you're selling plates, glassware or other fragile items, you need to pack them so they arrive undamaged. If you're mailing photos or items that can be easily bent or folded, you need to package them in a sturdy mailer, and mark "Do not bend, or fold" all over the package. I don't know about your mail person, but my mail lady likes to bend and fold everything so she can cram it all in that tiny mail box.

Take a few moments before you list any item to think about how you are going to mail it. Will your item fit in a small box or card stock mailer? Is it going to require lots of elaborate packing materials and sturdy corrugated boxes? The item you are selling is going to affect how you need to ship your item, and what you are going to charge for shipping.

eBay allows you several ways to charge shipping fees. You can choose flat rate, where everyone pays the same shipping charge no matter where they live. With this method if you set your shipping fee at $5.00 everyone would pay $5.00, whether they live in the same state as you, or 2000 miles away in Alaska or Hawaii. You can also choose "calculated shipping." With calculated shipping you enter the weight of your item when you list it, and eBay automatically calculates shipping charges to any destination. By using calculated shipping, someone living closer to you normally pays less for shipping, making your item more attractive to them.

eBay lets you choose several methods of shipping. Among the choices you can offer are first class, media mail, priority mail, or express mail. By offering choices buyers can elect a less expensive method of shipping, or chose a more expensive method that will get their item to them quicker.

One other obstacle you're going to bump up against is Free Shipping. eBay recommends that every seller should offer free shipping. They suggest that you absorb shipping and handling fees into your pricing. My thought is to see what other sellers are doing with similar items. If everyone else is offering free shipping for items similar to what you are selling then you should probably join the pack. If the majority of sellers are charging for shipping, I would suggest charging separately for shipping.

_____

eBay makes it easy for you to mail items.

You can print shipping labels directly from the item listing as soon as your buyer pays. To do this click **My eBay** at the top of the eBay page. Select **Sold** items in your selling manager. From here you can just go to the item you need to mail and click in the final column where it says sell similar. From the drop down menu select **print shipping labels**. From here you will be taken to the Print a shipping label page.

Fill in the weight and shipping method if they aren't already prepopulated for you. From there it's just a simple matter of selecting the options you want. You can add delivery confirmation, signature confirmation, and insurance.

I want to take a minute and define those last three terms:

Delivery confirmation means the mailman scans your package when he leaves it at your customer's house. It is proof your item was delivered. If you print your mailing label through eBay or PayPal, delivery confirmation is included for free with most options. If you mail your item at the Post Office you need to fill out a special form, and pay the fee (55 cents at this writing).

You want to include delivery confirmation with every item you sell. It keeps you and your buyer honest. The first thing eBay or PayPal are going to do if the buyer starts an item not delivered case is check delivery confirmation. If it shows delivered – you win. If there's no delivery confirmation, you lose because there is no way to prove your item was ever shipped, let alone delivered.

Signature confirmation is similar to delivery confirmation, except the buyer has to sign for your package in order to receive it. eBay and PayPal require signature confirmation on orders valued at over $200. You can include it with the label you print on line (the fee is $2.00). Once again, if you do your shipping at the Post Office you will need to fill out a separate form.

Insurance is an extra you can add to most packages. Insurance pays for damage or loss of your items while in transit. You don't have to purchase insurance. It is an option. What you do need to remember is: The seller is responsible for an item until it is delivered to the buyer in the condition you offered it for sale. If the item does not arrive, or arrives damaged, you are responsible.

Another thing to keep in mind is eBay does not allow sellers to charge buyers for insurance. You can build it into your shipping cost, or into the price of your item. You cannot charge for it as a standalone option.

The take away here is to carefully pack and ship every item you sell. Select the shipping options and extras that are important to you. If you decide not to insure every package, pick a price point $50 or $100 that you will buy insurance at and stick to that. This way you can limit your losses in case something unfortunate happens.

World Class Customer Service

On eBay the only thing a seller has is their good reputation.

Every time you sell an item the buyer has the opportunity to leave a feedback rating describing how well they thought you handled the transaction. They can leave a written comment about what they thought of your service and product. Buyers can also rate you in four categories including: item description, communication, how quickly you shipped their item, and cost of shipping.

It's called a five star rating system because they can give you from one to five stars in each category.

You would think getting four stars would be great. And it would in an ideal system, but in the eBay world four out of five stars can get you thrown off the site for poor customer service. eBay considers 4.8 to 5.0 as excellent customer service. Anything below 4.6 is considered unsatisfactory and you can lose your selling privileges.

So how do you give outstanding customer service on eBay?

It all starts with your listing. You need to accurately describe all of your items. If the item you're selling has any flaws you need to describe them completely, and add photographs where possible that highlight the problem areas.

Don't overcharge for shipping. Shipping charges are a really touchy issue on eBay right now. If customers even think you are overcharging for shipping many of them will leave you negative feedback in all four categories.

If you find yourself continuously receiving poor feedback for shipping then you may want to offer free shipping across the board. The reason for this is eBay automatically leaves you five star feedback if you offer free shipping.

Answer your email. If someone asks questions before or after the sale respond immediately.

Answer all complaints quickly. Don't hope they will magically go away. Apologize profusely. Accept all blame for the problem, even if it's clear you're not at fault. When someone writes me to say they haven't received their item, even when they paid just two days ago and its shipping to Japan, I start my email with:

"I'm sorry to hear you have not received your item yet. I did check my records. Your payment was received on ----, and it was mailed on ----. Normal delivery time is -----, so you should receive your item soon. Please keep me advised. Nick"

Notice – I don't go off on them for expecting the impossible. I apologize. I tell them the facts – when they paid, and when their item was mailed. Finally, I set expectations for delivery time, and I end by telling them it's ok to keep in touch.

Show concern. That's really all most people want.

What about requests for refunds?

My first job out of college was with Radio Shack Every time we had to give out a refund the manager would head for the back room as soon as the customer left and start screaming and ranting. Often times he would smash the returned item crashing it into the wall or the floor. I mention this only to point out how not to handle the situation.

When you're selling online and someone wants a refund, your reputation is at stake. The best thing you can do is apologize. Offer a full refund, including shipping both ways. The only alternative is facing the likelihood of receiving negative feedback. In the long run that's going to cost you more than any refund you can give.

Time to Get Started

We've covered how to find items to sell. How to list your items and how to price them for a quick sale

One final suggestion that may help you is to read through the seller profiles in the back of this book. Each of them shares a little bit about the seller's eBay journey. How they got started, where they see themselves going, and how their experiences may help you.

The first profile you're going to see is mine. It's pretty typical of most seller's experiences as they go through the ups and downs of selling on eBay.

I know you can do it. Every day thousands of people just like you are getting started selling on eBay. Thousands more want to give it a try, but are afraid to try. Don't be one of them.

Good luck and great selling.

Case Studies

Nick Collectibles

My story is typical of many eBay sellers.

I got my first taste of on line auctions in 1999. I had been following eBay and Yahoo Auctions for some time and one day I decided to take the plunge. I bought a couple baseball cards.

And then I bought some more, and some more. It was like an addiction.

Anyway, one thing led to another, and pretty soon I had this crazy idea that maybe I could sell some baseball cards, too. At this time I was buying "lots" of 1954 and 1955 Topps baseball cards thinking I could piece together a set. Many of the cards were lower grade, with creases and bruised corners, but they were a start.

Whenever I got a better card it went in my set. The other cards ended up in a cast off pile. As time went by I found myself with quite a few of these castoffs. And, they ended up being my first foray into auction selling.

My auctions were pretty unsophisticated at that time. Basically, I would scan a picture of the card, front and back, add a little description, and post it on eBay. Most of them I priced between $1.00 and $5.00 based on how mangled they were.

But the thing is - people bought them. Sometimes I even had bidding wars erupt, where they would jump from $1.00 to $10.00 and even $20.00 occasionally. Pretty cool stuff.

This went on for probably six months, and I was doing ok. I wasn't really making any money, because even though I was selling several hundred dollars-worth of cards a month, I was buying just as much or more. But it felt really good, because people were sending me money. Every day I received cash and checks in the mail, and dutifully I would package those baseball cards up, stuff them in an envelope, and mail them off to their new owners.

It was definitely fun. And to make it more interesting, back in those days, many people sent you cash, so many times, I had ten and twenty dollar bills falling out of all those envelopes.

Then one day I had one of those epiphany moments. I was perusing through the auction listings and caught sight of a guy selling an old magazine article (not a whole magazine, just one article taken from a magazine). It made me stop. And think. What kind of a nutcase would buy, or sell, a magazine article?

I read his description. I looked at his pictures. He was asking $10.00.

I needed to know a little more. So I looked at the other items he was selling, and he had about fifteen or twenty of these magazine articles for sale. Some of them had bids. A couple of them were over $20.00.

I looked at his sold history. And, over the past six months he had sold nearly one hundred magazine articles. Not bad for a few pieces of paper torn out of a musty old book.

I went back to selling my baseball cards. But over the next few weeks my thoughts kept wandering back to the guy selling magazine articles. I liked history. I liked books. It seemed like something I could do.

My first step into this new venture was to purchase a copy of Harper's Magazine from 1865. It had a good mix of articles. Some articles were on the Civil War and others on historical places and events.

My investment was a whopping $15.00. And, like just about all of the items I sell, I bought it on eBay.

When my issue of Harper's arrived I paged through it. Before I took it apart, I made a list of which articles I was going to sell, how I was going to describe them, and how much I was going to ask for them.

Anyway, to make a long story short, I sold most of those articles pretty quickly. My $15.00 investment quickly turned into $250.00. And like my venture with baseball cards, I found myself buying more and more, and still more books to break apart and sell.

Today I have over 6,000 items listed on eBay, and just over 10,000 on Amazon.

Over the past thirteen years I have completed nearly 30,000 sales as history-bytes on eBay alone. I'm just ending my first year of selling on Amazon, and have racked up close to 200 sales there. It's proving to be a tough nut to crack compared to eBay, but I will make it happen.

After being laid off in 2004, I jumped into eBay full time. I went from making $500 a month to $5000 a month.

Before doing this, I read everything written about eBay that I could get my hands on. I had someone design a custom template and eBay store interface for me. I plugged my picture into every auction listing hoping to build trust into my listings. I offered a "100% Money Back Guarantee – No Questions Asked."

I went from having 500 listings in my eBay store to maintaining almost 10,000 items listed for sale at any given time. I was listing 400 items each and every week, and I was mailing out nearly 150 packages every week.

It was more work than having a job. I don't think there was a single week that I clocked under 70 hours. It was a seven day work week.

And this is pretty much true of every full time eBay seller I have ever talked with or read about. It's a 24 / 7 job.

You get hooked on it.

Many of my best sales came about by accident. Others happened because of deliberate planning, and a whole lot of luck.

In growing my business I took a lot of chances.

I stretched the barrier every chance I could on pricing. Many of the sellers in my category were selling the same items I was selling for a whole lot less. I was asking $25.00 or $30.00, they were asking $5.00 or $10.00 for the same thing. I decided long ago to go for the gusto. My items have always sold better at a higher price.

I found myself trying a lot of new things.

One of my great successes was selling newspapers. I bought every bound volume I could of the Niles Weekly Register. It was one of the first real National newspapers in America. Over time I was able to assemble almost a complete run from 1811 to 1833.

From 1812 to 1815 they contained great accounts of battles and leaders in the War of 1812. I read through every paper, and listed them on eBay one by one. I included excerpts of battlefield accounts in all of my listings. Two of them on the burning of the White House went for about $100 each. Another, from 1811, contained a printing of the Declaration of Independence, side-by-side with Jefferson's notes for it. That one garnered $250.

I even tried bundling with a few of them. Two of our presidents, Thomas Jefferson and John Adams, died on July 4, 1826. Four papers were dedicated to their lives, an account of their deaths, and news of their funerals. These papers sparked some of the hottest bidding any of my auctions ever received. The final price they sold for was over $500.

Another time I was bidding on an 1840's copy of George Catlin's **Letters and Notes**. I lost the bid. It sold for over $500. But another seller emailed me she had a copy she was willing to part with for $200. I jumped on it, and sold the individual pictures for over $3500. It was a nice score, and brought me lots of new customers.

I stumbled across eight bound volumes of the **Annals of Congress** from the 1830's for $10 each. They were filled with news of the battle at the Alamo and Mexican troop movements in Texas. The Mormon exodus from Illinois and Missouri was discussed over and over again, along with many other popular topics of the day. Once again, I was able to sell individual pages about the Alamo and the Mormon's for $100 or more – each.

If I could tell sellers anything about eBay, it would be to develop a specialty that no one else is serving, and work it for all its worth.

Many of my customers have been with me since the first days I started selling on eBay. They know I'm always out there searching for new and unique things. And they appreciate that, and keep coming back to see what new articles I've discovered.

Over the years I've sold items to: the White House Historical Society, the Royal Museum in Jamaica, castles and historical societies all over the United States, Europe, Japan, China, Russia, Australia, and more. Hundreds of authors and publishers count on me for information when they are writing books, and illustrating magazine articles and books.

Museums buy illustrations and articles every day to augment their displays.

Probably the most off the wall sale I ever made was an article I found in a 1950's movie star magazine. There was a letter from a pregnant movie star to her unborn daughter. Fifty years later her daughter saw that article in one of my listings, and purchased a letter from her mom that she had never seen, or even knew existed.

In the thirteen years I've been selling on eBay technology has changed. People's wants and needs have changed. I now have my own website, digitalhistoryproject.com. I'm offering many of my more popular magazine articles as Kindle and Nook Books.

Who knows where your eBay journey will take you?

Jenny – Artist Showcase

Jenny was in her first year of college when the eBay bug struck her.

She had always had an artsy side. One of the things that intrigued Jenny about eBay was it allowed her to build an artist platform that could reach millions of people.

Two of her friends had opened eBay stores where they could showcase their art works. What they liked about eBay was the ability to include an artist biography on their "me" page. Each listing allowed them to expand on their biography, adding more details. They were also able to showcase each work with unlimited illustrations, and to describe the story behind each of their works.

Shortly after this Jenny opened her own store. She hired a professional to design her storefront, and put together a custom template to list her artwork with. She was determined everything had to be professional from the get-go. Her eBay career began with fifteen listings, all original paintings. She priced them reasonably, anywhere from $250 up to $1500 for her most expensive work, a giant 36" x 60" painting.

Sales were nonexistent the first few months. She can recall checking her sales every few hours the first week waiting for the magic to happen. It didn't. And, as the weeks began to drag into months she began having serious doubts about the whole idea. Her friends had both made sales their first month, and all of the waiting for a sale to happen gave her endless worries.

Several times she lowered her prices $50 and $100 at a time, but still no sales.

And then one day she received an email. It was a lady asking about one of her paintings. She wanted to know a little more about it, and she wanted exact dimensions to see if it would fit into a frame she had. That was an "ah-ha" moment for Jenny. She had given approximate dimensions in her listings, not thinking people needed exact sizes to fit frames they already had, or a particular space they wanted to display her art in.

After that she decided to take a good look at all of her listings, and ended up making several changes.

Of course she added the actual dimensions of each work. She talked more about the paintings themselves. She explained what she was feeling when she painted them, who her influences were during the period she painted them, the type of brush strokes she used, the subtleness of the colors, and symbolism she used in them.

She also gave suggestions about where they would look good. "A similar painting of mine hangs over the fireplace in a major corporate office." "Another painting in this series is the centerpiece of so-and-so's den." "The colors in this outdoor scene would go great in a rustic cabin setting."

She started including more feedback from people who liked her artwork – "reminiscent of," "made me think of," "the colors seemed to," "When I saw it, all I could think of was."

"I decided to get them thinking about where they could exhibit my paintings," said Jenny. "I wanted to get the internal conversation going, by including some of the emotions my paintings brought out in people looking at them."

Once she did this, customers started engaging her in more email conversations. And, from here she started to make more sales. "It was like people needed a little nudge," Jenny told me. "They wanted to know what my paintings were all about. And they wanted to know more about me both as a person and as an artist."

Another change she made was to add limited edition prints of some of her more popular works. She discovered people were more apt to jump in and buy her works for $50 or $100, than for $500 or $1000.

If Jenny could give other artists any advice, it would be "to be patient. It takes people time to find you on eBay, and it takes them more time to actually take the plunge and buy your works."

"While you're waiting for buyers to come along, make sure your profile is up to date. Write an exciting **me** page, telling about your artworks and any awards you've won. Make it personal and fun."

"Make sure all of your listings really talk up your offering. Include plenty of great quality pictures, and let people know its ok to contact you with questions."

Bill - Classic Mustangs

Bill's thing is cars.

You can figure that out as soon you start talking with him. Everything he says goes back to cars. Especially Mustangs. His first one was a 1966 convertible he bought when he was in his early twenties. It was green. Since then he's owned thirteen different Mustangs.

By day he's a corporate lawyer in a large insurance office. But nights and weekends, Bill is all about cars. He has a five car garage and he has three projects going just about all of the time.

Bill's entry into eBay was looking for parts to complete one of his cars. He needed a windshield wiper switch for a '68 Mustang and nobody local had one, so he turned to eBay. He found three of them on eBay, and snapped one up "at a pretty good price."

When he was looking for the wiper switch he discovered eBay had thousands of other Mustang parts, many that he always had trouble finding where he lived. Over the next few months he was drawn back to eBay several times, and was surprised how easy it was to find and buy just about any part he needed.

That got Bill thinking. Over the last twenty years he had filled several sheds with parts he'd taken from projects cars he stripped down to rebuild others. He did a little reading about how to sell on eBay, and talked with some friends who made occasional sales there.

His first sale was a mirror set for a 1971 Mustang – fifty bucks.

From that point on Bill was entirely jacked up about selling on eBay. Pretty soon he was listing twenty, even thirty parts a week. Many of them were selling at a pretty good price. What really surprised Bill though, was all of the emails people started sending him once they saw how many Mustang parts he was selling. They had to see what other goodies he might have stored away.

Bill soon found himself to be considered a "Mustang expert." Not only were people asking him if he had this or that part, "they were asking me for my advice," he said. "They wanted to know if I knew anything about body work, or how to replace this or that part."

Several times people contacted him to see if he was looking for project cars. Once he found himself traveling from a little town outside of Chicago all of the way to Bangor, Maine for a '65 Mustang he just had to have.

Another time he was offered a 1965 Pony Fastback. That one was in Wisconsin, so he didn't have to go quite so far for it.

According to Bill "the next logical step was to start selling cars." He sold his first one about two years ago – a '71 Mach One that he had completely restored. Since then he's sold three more cars in various stages of restoration.

"I'm finally doing what I always wanted to," says Bill. "Right now, I'm restoring two to three cars a year. eBay gives me a ready market for selling them. I think the longest it took to sell any of them was three weeks. The second one sold the first week."

But, "the best thing," according to Bill is the recognition. Once he joined the conversation, posting on automotive bulletin boards, it wasn't long until he became the "go-to guy" for all things Mustang. He's even written several articles for national magazines.

"Selling on eBay put me out there as an expert," says Bill. "Now I'm not that lawyer with the crazy fetish for cars! I'm 'Mr. Mustang.'"

"See you selling on eBay!" exclaims Bill.

Johnnie – Information products

Johnnie was crippled in a car accident nearly twenty years ago. Since then he's had to use a wheel chair to get around.

"Life hasn't been easy since then," admits Johnnie. "I get disability and there was a settlement from the accident that gave me some money to get by on. It's just I've always felt sort of useless since it happened.

"I was a construction worker, and it's not like there's much work for a guy in a wheel chair. Not in that line of work anyway."

Several years ago Johnnie read an e-book about selling information products on eBay. He bought it and several other e-books, too. Two of them had something called "resell rights" that allowed him to resell the books for himself on eBay or anywhere else he chose.

Johnnie decided it was something he could do.

His first attempts on eBay were really simple. He found some clip art of hundred dollar bills in a money clip, and put them in his listing, along with a few details telling everyone how much money they could make using the e-book system. Unsure what to charge, he decided inexpensive was the way to go. He priced his offering at 97 cents.

The first month Johnnie sold 33 copies of that e-book. He didn't make a whole lot of money after paying eBay, but he did see the potential.

Before long, Johnnie had an eBay store stocked with over two hundred e-books. At 97 cents each he was selling close to 500 e-books. That was still a long way from where he wanted to be. Johnnie decided there were only two ways he could grow his e-book business: 1) Sell more books, and 2) Charge more money.

His first move was to selectively raise prices. By this time several of his e-books had sold 100 copies or more. On each of these he raised his price to $5.99. All of the other books he re-priced between $2.99 and $4.99. He even featured five books at $19.99. For these five books, he made all new covers, and he rewrote the descriptions from the ground up.

The results surprised even Johnnie. "I still sold 400 books the month after I raised all those prices. I'd always thought a low price was the only reason people bought my e-books," said Johnnie. "I never really gave a thought to it until then. They were looking for the solutions my books brought them. They weren't thinking about the price!"

And, about those books he priced at $19.99. "I sold seven of them that first month," added Johnnie. "Seven!"

Nick Vulich

eBay Unleashed
A Beginner's Guide to Making Money on eBay

Copyright © 2013 by Nick Vulich

Getting Started with eBay

A re you struggling to get started with eBay? Are you wondering if you can really sell items, just by listing them on an online auction site? Would you like someone to hold your hand, and guide you through your first few listings?

This book can help you with all of this and more.

I've been selling on eBay for thirteen years now. And, for five of those years I have made a full time living just by selling magazines and books through my eBay store.

Some years, I've made as much as $40,000 to $50,000.

Most years, when I do eBay part time to supplement my regular gig, I still make $20,000 to $25,000. For most of us that is enough extra money to make the house payment, utilities, cable, and even have enough left over to drive a brand new car every other year.

As you can see, eBay has been a great thing for me financially. When I'm in between jobs, I can step things up and make a full time living. When I want to slow it down a little, I just pull back on my new listings, and leave my eBay store alone to run on auto-pilot so all I need to do is mail out my items as they are sold and paid for.

What I want to do in this short guide is show you how you can set up an eBay business of your own.

Whether you want to make a few hundred dollars per month, or build a powerful eBay store that can make you several thousand dollars per month, I will give you all of the information you need to make it happen.

What I am going to do is take you step-by-step through setting up your eBay account, setting up a PayPal account, and placing your first listings on eBay. Then we will talk a little bit about advanced selling strategies, and different methods that can help you increase your earnings.

Unlike other books about selling on eBay that drag on for 300 to 400 pages, I've deliberately kept this book short – under sixty pages.

Let's face it if you're like most people you already have a full time job. You don't have time to read through a whole bunch of filler to find the few gems you need to get started.

Deciding What to Sell

Probably the hardest thing for most people is deciding what they want to sell on eBay.

My suggestion is to start with everyday items you have around the house. If your family is anything like mine, you have plenty of extra stuff stashed away in every nook and cranny. My wife and kids have been planning a yard sale for five years now, and all of that stuff is filling up the garage. The kids have old toys, unused video games, videos, and CD's everywhere.

Chances are many of those items are things other people will want.

Take a look at a few of them, and then search for them on eBay. It's going to amaze you how much people are willing to pay for some old books or CD's. Just because your kids moved up to the newest greatest video game system doesn't mean someone else out there wouldn't be happy to have that old game console, especially if you could package it with five or ten games.

Another advantage of starting out by selling items you already have around the house is you can get started without investing a single penny. This way you can test the waters for free, and see for yourself, if selling on eBay is something you would like to pursue.

Setting up your eBay account

S etting up your eBay account is easy to do, fast, and best of all free.

When you go to the main eBay screen, in the upper left hand corner, you will see "Hi! Sign in or Register." Click on that, and it will bring you to a screen that says "Getting started with eBay."

Getting started really is as easy as it looks. Enter your first and last name, and email address.

Next you need to supply a user name. This is how people are going to know you on eBay. I suggest you give this some careful thought. A good user name should convey some type of information about what you sell.

If you have an idea about the type of products you intend to sell, try to put a spin on it to create a unique user name. If you are selling videos, you could use the name videostogo or sportsvideos. Both of them convey a sense of your business. If you plan on selling movie posters, you could try movieposters or moviemagic. Again, you can get a feel for the type of items you sell by looking at the username.

A word of caution here, eBay currently has over 250 million users so many of the names you think of are going to be taken already. Some simple ways of using the name you like are to add hyphens or underscores. For example, you can try using moviemagic as movie-magic or movie_magic. Sometimes it will work, sometimes other users have tried the same trick.

If you're totally stumped, don't sweat it. eBay allows you to change user names every thirty days.

Finally, pick a password, and you are a member of the eBay community.

The next step is to update your information, so you can get set up to start selling. To do this, click Sell in the upper right hand corner of the eBay screen.

That will take you to the Update Your Information.

Go ahead and update your information, including street address and phone number. Make sure you use the correct information your post office uses as this address will be used to determine shipping charges when you buy or sell items.

Next, select a secret question to help secure your account, and click continue.

The next screen you see is going to give you lots of great information about selling on eBay. Take a moment to bookmark it so you can return for more information as needed.

Set Up Your PayPal Account

P ayPal is the fastest and easiest way to get paid on eBay.

Setting up a PayPal account is an essential part of becoming an eBay seller. The good news is getting started with PayPal is fast and free.

To sign up you need to visit https://www.paypal.com. This will take you to the "Sign up for PayPal screen."

It is automatically set for the United States and English as the language. Click on the dropdown boxes to change the settings if you need to.

Next you are asked to select whether you want a personal or business account. Select the **business account**. You will need to upgrade to it anyway as you continue to sell more items.

The next screen asks you to pick a payment solution.

For now, choose the standard plan with no monthly charges. The other plans are targeted at more advanced sellers who have online stores or shopping carts.

Click **Get Started** in the Standard box.

The next screen offers you the opportunity to Create New Account or Log in. Click on **Create New Account.**

Another screen pops up asking you to choose your country and language. Click on the dropdown boxes if you need to make any corrections, and select **Create New Account.**

That will bring up a new box for you to start entering your personal information.

Go ahead and fill in your answers. When you're finished enter the security code and click on continue.

That will bring up the next screen.

Go ahead and fill in the requested information. If you have a website you want to add go ahead and type in the URL, otherwise you can leave this box blank. For category and sub-category scroll through and pick out the ones that are closest to what you plan on selling.

The following four questions will probably be the toughest ones to fill out when you are just getting started.

1. *What will your average monthly payment volume be?*
2. *What will your average transaction amount be?*
3. *What percentage of your annual revenue will come from online sales?*
4. *Do you sell on eBay?*

It's ok to guess.

The odds are starting out your average monthly payment volume will be less than $5,000. Unless you're selling electronics or other more expensive items, your average transaction amount will most likely be under $25.00. If you are only going to be selling items online, choose 75%-100% for the percentage of your annual revenue that will come from online sales. If you have a brick-and-mortar location, or sell at flea markets, you can estimate the percentage you think you will sell online. Select **Yes** where it asks Do You Sell on eBay.

After this you will be directed to the final page requesting your personal information. Go ahead and fill it out. Select continue, and you will be taken to a screen that says you are all signed up with PayPal.

Congratulations! You are now able to sell on eBay, and collect your payments with PayPal.

The good news is: The boring stuff is over. Now we can get down to the business of selling.

Before You Start Selling

I honestly believe you have to be an eBay buyer first, before you can become a good eBay seller.

If you've never bid on an auction, and returned to the site repeatedly to check on your progress for the days and minutes leading up to its close, you have no idea what your customers are feeling. If you've never waited anxiously for the item you won to arrive, you aren't going to really understand why quick shipping is so important.

The fact is: If you haven't been an eBay buyer, you're going to have trouble relating to customers.

If you've never purchased anything on eBay before my advice is to wait a few weeks before you even think about starting to sell.

You need to start buying first.

It doesn't have to be anything expensive. You can buy a few books, some videos, a case for your phone, whatever you choose. Just start buying some stuff.

Here's one way you can approach it.

Pick a few items with Buy-it-Now (where you can click and it's yours). Bid on a few auctions, where you actually have to watch, and see if you are winning. As soon as you win the bid, go into the auction and pay with PayPal. Get a feel for working with the invoices buyers send to you.

When your items arrive, don't just tear them open. Take a few minutes to examine each package. Did the seller pack your item in a box or an envelope? Did they ship it first class, priority, or media mail? What about the label? Did they write it out by hand, and use stamps, or did they print a professional label with the postage printed on it?

Next take a few moments to carefully open each package, and note how your items are packed inside. Did the seller use bubble wrap? Did they wrap your item in newspaper? Or was your item just tossed half-assed into the box?

Finally, did they include an invoice? A thank-you note? Or any request for you to contact them should you be unhappy with your purchase?

Really think about it for a minute with each package you receive. How did the sellers packaging make you feel? If they included a note, did that make it a more pleasurable buying experience?

Your First Listing

It's time to create your first listing. To get started click the Sell button in the upper right hand corner. That will bring up the Tell us what you sell screen.

Enter a short description of your item, a UPC, ISBN, or VIN. Once you have been selling for a while you may want to visit the box just below this where it says Sell with a template. (A template makes selling easier because it is prepopulated with all of the information you normally use in a listing. When you sell with a template it allows you to work quicker and smarter. All you need to do is add the item specific details and pictures, because everything else is there for you.)

For our example, type books into the box and you will be taken to the Find a matching category button.

This gives you the opportunity to choose a sub-category for your book. You can check on one of the categories you see listed to choose the correct subsection within books. The Browse categories button allows you to search for a new category if books are not what you wanted. The Recently used categories button will show all of the categories you have previously used.

Go ahead and select Antiquarian and select continue at the bottom.

After this you will be taken to the Create your listing page. This is where you will create the rest of your listing.

Most of this form is pretty self-explanatory. At the top it shows you the category you are selling in, and then you have the opportunity to select a store category. This doesn't apply when you are just getting started and don't have an eBay store so you can just skip by it for now. The same goes for inventory. Skip by it for now.

The title box allows you 88 characters to describe your item. Choose your words carefully.

A great title is loaded with relevant search terms related to what you are selling. For example, if you are selling an IPod some of the keywords that you would want to include are: IPod, 8GB, 16GB, 32 GB, new in box, refurbished, reconditioned by Apple, warranty, black, white.

You want to make sure you get every possible search term you can fit into the 88 characters you are allowed. It doesn't have to be a complete sentence. It doesn't have to make sense. It just has to have a great combination of keywords.

Here are several great titles running right now:

> Apple IPod touch 4th generation white (8 GB) New Screen Replaced refurbished
> Refurbished Apple IPod Touch 4th Generation White 8GB with Accessories
>Apple IPod Touch 4th Generation Black 64GB Mint with charger/case bundle

That's the way you want to do it. Pack every keyword you can in there.

Next you are offered the opportunity to add a subtitle. In most cases you're going to want to skip this. It costs $1.50 per listing period, way too much money for the value you are going to get out of it.

What a subtitle does is allow you to add more information about your listing that people can see before they click into it. The downside is, the information in a subtitle is not searchable, so it does not help potential buyers find your items. If you're selling something expensive or unique, the subtitle can sometimes help clinch the sale. You do need to be careful because if you're item doesn't sell on the first try, every time you relist it you're going to be charged another $1.50.

Item condition description is a new field I really like. It shows up at the top of your listing, and can help prevent a lot of misunderstandings if you list any faults there.

To fill in the rest of this section, just follow the prompts. If you don't know the answer for one, or are unsure how to answer leave it blank.

Origin and country of manufacture let you add the region and country of manufacture. This can be important when you are selling your item internationally. Below that there is a spot for you to add item specifics if you have any other details you want to put out there. I have never used this one.

To add pictures just click on the yellow box and choose the pictures you want to upload from your computer. eBay allows you to upload up to twelve pictures for free. Use as many pictures as you need to present your item. It is recommended that your pictures are at least 1600 pixels on the longest or tallest end. You can resize pictures in Paint or a similar program. If you are using a lot of pictures I would suggest a program such as Adobe LightRoom. Using it I can resize several hundred pictures in less than five minutes.

Next you need to add your item description. eBay allows you unlimited space for your description, so be sure to tell everything needed to entice potential buyers.

A good description should include all details related to your item. Describe everything accurately. Be sure to note any flaws, no matter how small (include pictures where possible). Some of the things you should mention are: brand, model number, dimensions, color, special features, and any other factors relevant to your item.

The listing designer allows you to dress up your listing if desired. Don't waste your dime. The visitor counter lets you track the number of people looking at your item. It's a good way of discovering how popular your item is.

After this you are offered the option of listing your item as an online auction or as fixed price. Auction is just like it sounds. Potential buyers can bid on your item, and the highest bidder wins. A Fixed Price listing is just like buying from a local store. You price the item, and the first person willing to pay the price gets the item.

There are a couple spins on each of these you need to know before you list your item.

With auctions you have the ability to add buy-it-now. What that means is you set two prices – one price that bidding starts from, and the other, the buy-it-now price, which allows potential buyers to purchase your item without bidding.

Fixed Price sales allow you to set a price, and then add something called best offer. Best offer lets you to accept offers from your customers. Most customers send their offer using the best offer form. Others like to test the waters and email you first with the price they have in mind. A lot of the customers who email me first, preface the conversation by saying they have five or six items they are considering, would I accept so much for each of them. At that point we can deal back and forth some and I can adjust the best offer parameters so it will accept their offers when they put them in. (Quick note here: Always make sure to complete your transactions through eBay. Completing sales off site is against eBay policy, and can get your account suspended).

Duration allows you to select the length of your listings. Seven days is standard for auctions, but you have the option of running it for one, three, five, seven, and ten days. Fixed price listings can run for thirty days, or good till cancelled (which means it automatically relists until the item sells, or you cancel the listing).

Where it tells you to decide how to be paid, select PayPal and add the email address that is linked to your PayPal account. This is where all your invoices will be issued from, and all payment notices will be sent to this address as well.

With shipping, you have two different sections to fill out. One is for shipping in the United States, and the other is for international shipping.

You have the option of specifying flat rate (everybody pays the same amount) or calculated (shipping is determined by where the customer lives). I always use flat rate shipping. It just works out easier with the type of items I sell. Most of them are less than six ounces and easily fit in stay flay mailers.

You are also allowed to pick different levels of shipping – including media mail, first class, priority mail, flat rate priority mail, and express mail. Be aware that in certain categories, such as books, sellers are required to offer one shipping service for $4.00 or less. If you decide to offer free shipping, check the free shipping box to the far right.

At the very bottom of the shipping section you need to select a handling time. Keeping your handling time under three days will keep customers happy because they will receive their packages sooner. If you are a member of the Top Rated Seller program or aiming towards it, eBay requires you to offer one day handling time.

I've always offered international shipping. Many weeks a third of my customers are international buyers so without them, I would have much weaker sales. And the truth is selling internationally is no harder than shipping within the United States. If you use any of the shipping tools available in PayPal, eBay, Stamps.com, or Endicia they will take care of the majority of work on the customs forms for you. If you take your mail to the Post Office have them walk you through the customs forms the first few times.

eBay started something new this year to make international shipping even easier. It's called the Global Shipping Program. To enable your item for international shipping click in the box next to Global Shipping Program and eBay will take care of everything else. When any of your items sell internationally they will charge your customer for shipping and customs fees and send you a U S address to mail your items to. Once your item arrives at the eBay shipping center in the United States they are responsible for delivery to your international customer.

It's as simple as mailing to a U S address.

The final section on the first page for listing your item is titled Other things you'd like buyers to know.

You have the opportunity to add any buyer restrictions here. An example would be restricting bidders who have two or more non-paying strikes against them. My suggestion would be to be as lenient as possible. Better to give people the benefit of the doubt than drive away potential customers.

If you're charging sales tax (and you should be), this is where you set up the tax rates for your state.

Return Policies are set here as well. eBay does not require you to accept returns, but it is strongly encouraged. If you accept refunds, you can specify a time frame for them – normally either fourteen or thirty days. There is also a box for you to spell out your return policy. Spell out all of the details.

Tell customers if you have any special requirements or restrictions regarding returns, how long your return period is, and who pays return shipping. If you need to be contacted prior to the item being returned, tell people here.

eBay released a new return program this year to streamline shipping. If you opt into it returns are handled automatically through their system. My thought is to give this one a little extra thought. A lot of times you can prevent returns or misunderstandings with a quick email. If you use eBay's automated returns program you're going to miss that opportunity to save your sale and keep your customer happy.

Finally there is one last box at the bottom of this section where you can specify additional checkout details. Examples would be forms of payment accepted. If they are making multiple purchases, you can ask buyers to wait for an adjusted invoice before paying. This way you can combine shipping, and have them pay for all of their purchases at the same time. It will make shipping and tracking a whole lot easier.

And, way down at the very bottom, just before you click continue, eBay shows you your fees for this auction so far.

At the top of the second page eBay makes their pitch for all of their upsells. My best advice would be to pass on all of them. It's an extra cost that isn't going to pay you back in most cases. At the bottom of this page you can review the total fees you owe. Click on submit and your item will be listed.

It sounds like a lot of details, but after you do it two or three times you will be a pro.

Some Quick Words of Advice

Now that we've talked about the basics of how to sell I want to share some tips and tricks that might make selling easier for you.

How to Use Auctions

Auctions used to be the way to sell on eBay. Over the last few years, the market has moved more towards fixed price offerings where people can just click on the item they want, and buy-it-now.

The new rule for auctions is to use them when you have something unique, and you are unsure of the price it may bring. An example here would be a Superman Number 1 Comic in less than prime condition. You know it's going to sell, and you probably have a good idea of the range it will sell in, but you want to take a shot at the moon.

There are two pricing strategies with auctions:

1) Start at 99 cents and let the market set the price. This will attract the maximum number of bidders, as potential buyers jump in trying to pick up a bargain. If things go right, this is a great way to get the most money from an item, because if you can spur a bidding war between two or more buyers, the sky is the limit. Unfortunately, in today's market, this can be a dangerous strategy. If you can't spark the bidding war you were hoping for you're going to be in for some major disappointments.

2) Start your item at the price you need to get, and add a buy-it-now where you can still score a higher price if somebody bite's on it. This strategy will save a lot of heartache and grief if the bidders you were hoping for never materialize. One example from my selling, and I will let it go. I had and 1858 county history of Scott County. It was the only one listed anywhere on line, and they normally sold for $300 to $400. My cost was $181, and I started it for $9.99 with no reserve. I used all of the upgrades, bold listing, highlighted and featured in category, and no reserve price (meaning the item would sell to the highest bidder, no matter how low). My listing upgrades cost nearly $20. The item sold for $18.81 (shipping included). Lesson learned: Don't set yourself up to lose money.

Auction Timing

There's a lot of talk out there about auction timing, specifically the best time to start and end your auctions. My thought is – that's all it is, a bunch of talk. People log onto eBay constantly, from work, from home, or on the go with eBay Mobile.

It's silly to assume any day or any specific time of the day is better than any other. People are logging in from all over the world to check in on your auction. The only part of this advice I will buy into is you want to run your auction so it goes through at least one weekend. This will assure you the maximum number of people have the opportunity to view your auction.

Try not to end your auction on a holiday. I've had holidays where I've had really good sales, but most of them have been disappointing. Traffic is normally lower during holidays because people spend more time on the road, and with their families. If you must be on eBay on a holiday, be a buyer, not a seller.

Research Everything Before You Sell

If you're not sure how to price an item, check eBay to see how many are currently up for sale, and how much they have sold for in the last few weeks.

I sold sports cards back in the early 90's. Every dealer waited for the new *Beckett's Price Guide* to come out each month to see how much their items were worth so we could adjust the price before the next sports card show. The good news with eBay is all the information is right there. There's no need to wait for the latest price guide to come out.

If you're in doubt, do an advanced search on eBay. You can do this by visiting the search box, and clicking advanced at the right end of the search box.

This will bring up the advanced search box.

Scroll down a ways until you come down to the section that says search including. Check by **Completed listing**. This is going to pull up accurate information on how many listings were completed over the last two weeks. This way you don't have to do any guessing. In just a matter of minutes you can see how many listings sold, how many didn't, and the prices they sold for.

Take a look at several of the listings that sold for the highest price. Make some notes on the item condition, the title, the description, and any pictures the seller used.

No use reinventing the wheel. This is information you can use in your listing, so be sure you note the price ranges and keywords (if any) that were used. All you have to do is put your own spin on it, improve the listing where possible, and put your item up for sale.

Develop Your Own Niche

A lot of people sell everything but the kitchen sink, and wonder why their business just seems to stall out.

The fact is repeat customers are the backbone of every business, online or offline. You need to give customers a reason to come back. The way to do this is to focus on a certain product line or category.

Books are a broad category. Children's books or fantasy / science fiction are sub-categories customers have a keen interest in. If you develop a reputation for stocking the largest selection of children's books from long out-of-print to the newest releases, customers will keep coming back to check your store out. They will recommend you to friends and help grow your business for you.

Take the time to build your own niche, and become an expert in it.

Buy Low, Sell High

On eBay you make your money when you buy your inventory, not when you sell it.

It sound's contrary to popular belief, but it's true. If you pay too much for an item, you can't make your money back by raising the price.

No one cares how much money you have invested in an item. They're going to pay you what it is worth to them. Not a penny more.

Let's take the Pawn Stars as an example. Every week customers come in with old guns, toys, posters, and other mementos that mean more to them than they are worth. Rick or Cory will call in an expert to price the item, and he will tell them it's worth $500. And, yet, the seller will demand $1000, because it's worth that much to them. As a result, there's no sale.

Don't let this happen to you!

Don't fall in love with any items. Only buy something if you are sure you can make money when you go to resell it.

Accept Returns

Returns are a normal part of doing business. If you really want to "fire up" your eBay business, add these seven words to every listing **100% Money Back Guarantee – No Questions Asked**. Despite the fact that most people shop on the internet, many of them are still afraid to take a chance on an **unknown seller – YOU**. So why not eliminate that fear upfront, and let people know you are happy to accept returns.

My return policy for history-bytes is posted right there in every listing –

*Here at history-bytes we understand buying things sight unseen on the internet can be a little scary at times. For that reason we offer a **100%***

Money Back Guarantee – No Questions Asked. *If you are unhappy for any reason you may return your item for a full refund, including shipping both ways.*

Any guesses on how many people have taken me up on that offer? Eleven. In thirteen years of selling on eBay, and 29,487 transactions I've refunded exactly eleven sales.

My suggestion is: Don't sweat refunds. Even if a customer writes demanding a refund, it doesn't mean that's what they really want. Often time it just means you need to tell them a little more about what they bought.

Here's a sample of the email I send to all of my customers who ask about retuning an item:

Sorry to hear you're not happy with your item. Here at historybytes customer satisfaction is very important to us. I will be happy to take your item back. You can return it to …

At this point one of two things is going to happen. The customer is going to email you to let you know the item is on its way back, or they're going to email you with the real reason they want to return it.

I sell old magazine articles removed from bound magazines. Over the years I've had at least 100 people tell me they're missing a page or it wasn't what they expected. But after I tell them "I will be happy to take the item back," just about every one of them has told me, it's ok, they want to keep it. Some of them just want to ask a few more questions about the item, and then they are happy with it.

The truth is most people just want to be listened to. Sure some people will be totally unreasonable and demand a refund no matter what. Give it to them, and move on.

It's OK to Fire Bad Customers

Some people are going to email back and forth forever. They're going to pick at your item, and question everything. They want extra pictures, or guarantees it will work for an application your item isn't made for. When I get a potential customer like this, I normally email them and suggest this probably isn't the right item for them if they have all of those unanswered questions, and politely suggest they shop elsewhere.

It prevents customer service hassles after the sale, and wards off potential negative feedback.

Add Video to Your Listings

Very few people use video in their item descriptions. Yet **a good video can increase your sales 25% or more**. I recently added video to my items, and I've seen a slight increase in sales so far. I have Professor Puppet explain to people different ways they can use my items. It's humorous, and gets the point across without being pushy. Click here to see my video.

I've seen video used effectively many times by sellers. Here are a few ideas how you can add video to your listings:

1) Show how to use an item
2) Show people having fun or solving a problem using your item

3) Introduce yourself and your business

4) If you sell something that needs to be installed, include a step-by-step video showing how easy it is to do.

If you decide to add video to your listings YouTube offers the easiest method. All you need to do is upload your video to YouTube. Once you have done that, click on **share**, and choose the **embed option**. Be sure to check the use **old embed code** box. Then highlight the html code and paste it into your auction where you would like the video to play

Don't Use Negative Language

Don't be a Negative Nelly. Some sellers put all sorts of disclaimers in their listings. They tell you you're entering into a legal contract when you make a bid, and you are obligated to follow through and make payment. At the same time, they feel obligated to point out they don't take returns, it's the buyers responsibility to be sure the item will work for their intended application, and they're too busy to waste time answering questions.

The point is: Don't make it hard for people to buy from you. Don't give them a reason to buy from someone else.

Cross Sell for Extra Sales

Be sure to tell potential buyers you have similar or complimentary products available for sale. A lot of the articles I offer for sale are part of a series. I always make sure to let people know this is part one of a three part series, and to be sure and check my other listings so they can get the full story. Oftentimes one person will buy the entire series.

You can do the same thing if you are selling digital cameras or cell phones. Let people know you offer accessories in your other listings. They're going to buy chargers, cases, and extra memory somewhere. Why not help them buy it from you?

Tell Stories

Take a chance now and then. If you have a unique item, tell a story about it. Let people know how you came to get it, about the previous owner, or about all of the cool things you can do with it.

One time I had a set of **The Annals of Congress** from 1832 to 1836. These were some really cool books detailing congressional proceedings, and what made these copies really special was – they were stamped Congressional Library, meaning Senators and Congressman from that day had probably used them. That means Abraham Lincoln, Daniel Webster, even Davy Crockett could have thumbed through them.

You've got to admit, that makes a pretty cool story. Every time I sold a section from one of them I featured the Congressional Library stamp and played up the possible associations. Many of the pages sold for $50 to $100 each.

Other sellers craft stories about how great-great grandpa carried this custom tooled Bible during the different campaigns he served in while in the Civil War or World War I, and what a great comfort it was to him, and all the stories he was said to have told afterwards while showing it to everyone he came across.

A good story can build interest in your item. A great story can make your item go viral and spark more and higher bids. You can't craft them for every item, but try it once or twice a month and see what happens.

Listing Templates

A great listing template can help you build your brand, and increase sales faster than anything else you do on eBay. A poorly designed template can do just the opposite.

If you decide to go the custom template route, don't be tempted by flash, animation, or sound bites. While they might look nice, they slow down your load time, distract viewers from your message, and irritate them by blaring strange sounds.

A good template design has plenty of white space. It has a well-placed title at the top, and the ability to add multiple pictures. It should have a badge saying "Money Back Guarantee" if you offer one. And, it should contain all of the basic information you normally have in a listing, so you can just plug in the added details pertinent to each listing.

Other template disasters I've experienced are:

1) Dark letters on a dark background (where you can hardly read the words)

2) Static backgrounds where your description scrolls up and down as you move through the page. It's distracting and hard to read.

3) Animated figures fluttering across the page. They're irritating, and don't add any value to your listing.

Templates also create other unexpected problems.

Some sellers have suggested eBay's new Cassini search has problems displaying listings that start with html code. So if you have a fancy listing header or a template design with html code at the beginning it's possible your items may not come up in search.

Another issue deals with mobile search. Right now slightly over one third of internet purchases are made on a mobile device or phone. Going forward that number is expected to reach fifty percent or better. What happens is when eBay looks for items to display in a mobile search they routinely ignore listings with embedded pictures or extensive html code.

See the *Catch 22* here. You want your listings to look good, but by dressing them up you may be keeping one-third to one-half of your potential buyers from finding your listing.

The best advice I can give you is to keep your listings *plain Jane*. Resist the urge to dress them up and you should experience greater sales.

Sell Light Items

Your life will be a lot easier if you sell light items that are easy to ship. Right now eBay is pushing all of their sellers to offer free or reduced shipping. It's a whole lot cheaper to do this with light items. It's even better if no special packing or handling is required. Look for items you can put in an envelope or box and be done with it.

Automate Shipping

Always use eBay and PayPal tools to ship your items. Doing so provides you with professionally printed labels, and assures you that you don't have any addressing snafus (because the customer address is prepopulated when you print the form).

Another advantage of using these tools is the tracking information is automatically uploaded into each of your items so you don't have to do it manually. This way customers can go into the auction details section and pull up all of their tracking info; they don't have to bother you to ask for a shipping update.

Two other great shipping tools are Stamps.com and Endicia. Both of them can import your sales information directly from eBay, and post tracking information back into your listings.

I use the upgraded edition of Stamps.com. It has a basic $15.99 per month, but it means I never have to go to the office. I do a lot of international business, and if you use the PayPal or eBay shipping tools, they only allow you to ship international packages by Priority or Express Mail. Using Stamps.com I can ship international items by First Class (which is a whole lot cheaper, especially with the recent Postal rate hikes), and print the Customs Label right there on my Shipping Label.

Let Customers Help You Sell

Add some of your feedback to your listings. If you've got some awesome feedback comments that relate directly to how customers are using your item, or how it has changed their lives, include that feedback in your listing – either set apart at the top of your listing or somewhere in the body of the description.

People believe it more when someone else tells them. Solicit customer feedback or testimonials and use them to sell your items.

Offer Shipping Discounts

Help customers spend more money with you.

Let customers know they can get free or reduced shipping on additional items. It won't work every time, but many customers will take the time to scan your offerings to see what other items they can find. Sometimes I upsell two or three items, other times I've had customers buy forty or fifty items all because they got started trying to save $2.67 on shipping.

Don't underestimate the power of a discount. $2.67 might not sound like much to you, but it might be just the added incentive for someone else to find another item or two.

Select the Right Category

Most eBay buyers use the search feature to find what they are looking for. However, statistics show roughly 30% of buyers choose to browse in categories when they are shopping on eBay. If you're not in the right place when they're looking, you're going to lose the sale almost one third of the time.

When I'm looking for a book, I normally enter the title of the book that I'm looking for or the topic. But there are times I search the categories too. If I want a book on the Spanish American War or Civil War I still search on those titles, but then I drill down into the categories afterwards, and narrow my search down to nonfiction or antiquarian. If your book isn't listed there, it's off my radar.

List for Seven Days

eBay offers you the option to list your auction items for one, three, five, seven, or ten days. Seven days is the time period that eBay starts with in each listing, and it is the optimal time frame for most items.

You can use a shorter time frame – one or three days, if you are trying to move something with a short life span such as concert or sports tickets. You may also use this option if you have a lot of inventory on an item that is selling briskly. Several years ago my wife scored a ton of Bedazzlers at a local fabric store. They were selling as quickly as I could list them, so I offered different time durations as I listed them. I had auctions running for three days, five days, and seven days, along with fixed priced listings, and they were all selling like crazy. It helped move our inventory faster.

The ten day listing is great for when you have a really special item. With the ten day listing you can run it over two weekends, and build maximum interest in it. There is an extra twenty cent fee for the ten day listing, but it is well worth it when used properly.

Skip the Listing Upgrades

Every time you list an item, eBay is going to try to upsell you all of their fancy upgrades – bold, subtitle, value pack. Using any of these features is going to suck up your hard eared profits. Listen to these charges: subtitle $1.50 – UK site visibility .50 – Bold $4.00.

The only time you should even consider any of these is if you're selling something really special, or very expensive. Then you might want to add the subtitle feature. Buyers can't search it, but the extra information you add there might get them to click in to visit your pictures and description.

Don't Use a Reserve Price

People want to know they have a chance to win your item. A starting price of 99 cents with a reserve makes people think your item is over-priced. If you're afraid to start at a low price, start your item at the lowest price you are willing to accept. The chances of selling your item will be much better.

Only Accept PayPal

Ninety-nine percent of your buyers are going to pay with PayPal. Don't worry about the other one percent. You're always going to get people who want to wire you money, or pay with Western Union. And, there are few holdouts that are still afraid to share credit card info on line, so they insist on sending checks or money orders. Go ahead and let them pay that way (just be aware, eBay policy won't let you say you accept checks or money orders in your listing).

Free Shipping Isn't Always the Answer

eBay is on this rant right now where they want every seller to offer free shipping.

Don't let yourself be forced into offering free shipping without considering how it will impact your profitability. Postal rates just went up (as of January 27, 2013). They are going up again before the end of 2013. Make sure you know the new rates. If you are shipping packages internationally the price of a five ounce package to most of Europe skyrocketed from $4.87 to $12.00 or $13.00.

Take a careful look at your costs and what your competition is doing before you make any decisions on offering free shipping. If most of the other sellers offering similar items are offering free shipping you may have to offer it too, just to be competitive. But, don't do anything until you consider how it impacts your bottom line. Remember, you're in this to make money, not to please eBay.

Customer Service is Everything

To be truly successful on eBay you need to be able to play well with the others.

Potential buyers are going to email you at all hours of the day and night with all sorts of crazy questions. Many of them ask questions they would already know the answer to if they bothered to read your listing. But, as a responsible member of the eBay community, you can't tell them that. You need to play nice and respond something like this, "Thank-you for inquiring about my auction. It is a great widget in super condition. To answer your question…"

See how I did that. The key to offering great customer service is to start every email off by saying "thank-you." It gives customers a warm fuzzy feeling about doing business with you. After that just restate their question, and then answer it. Be sure to mention several times it is a great widget, and they will really enjoy it.

Address complaints the same way. Start off with "thank-you," and then you can address their concern.

Always Ship with a Tracking Number

Things happen. Items get lost in the mail. Customers receive your item and misplace it, or forget all about receiving it. Some may even lie, and tell you it never arrived. Tracking numbers keep everyone honest, and offer positive proof your item was mailed and delivered. Without a tracking number, eBay and PayPal will always side with the buyer if an unpaid items case is opened.

As you begin selling more items and become a Top Rated Seller, one of the requirements is to upload tracking information on over ninety percent of your sales. If you do it from the start you won't have to make any adjustments later.

Don't waste space in your title

I'm constantly amazed by the number of people who waste the valuable real estate in their title. eBay gives you 88 characters to get your message across. You can't afford to waste even one of them, and yet every day I see things like "LQQK," or somebody wasting those valuable characters using adjectives like super, awesome, great, and fantastic.

The purpose of your title is to drive people to your auction. You need to load it with keywords that are going to help people find your item. Don't waste a single character. Be sure to include model number, brand, condition, dates, anything your buyer is going to look for.

And, one last thought – Your title doesn't even have to make any sense. It just has to include the correct keywords.

Use Best Offer

Use best offer in all of your fixed price listings. Yes, you're going to receive some lowball offers, but overall, you're going to find yourself accepting more offers than you turn down. If you're only concern is not wanting to be inundated with lowball offers, use the automated tools, and you will only see the offers that meet your preset criteria.

From my experience one third to one half of your items are going to sell at full price. The rest are going to sell using best offer.

Use Buy-it-Now in Your Auctions

Many people are willing to pay extra to get the item they want -**NOW**. A lot of people don't want the frustration of having to bid, and wait to see if they win. By adding buy-it-now to all of your auctions, you can solve this problem for them, and make it easier for them to do business with you.

From my experience, about one in ten auctions will close with a buy it now. eBay requires you to have at least a ten percent difference between your starting price and your buy it now price. My thought is you should shoot for much more. I start most of my auctions at $9.99, and set my buy-it-now price at $25.99.

Test the waters and see what works best for you.

Keep Testing New Things

No one ever made any money or grew their business without trying new things. You need to test new items. Try new selling methods.

My thought is you need to constantly be stretching your business model. Over the years I've sold thousands of videos, hundreds of pieces of clothing purchased from garage sales and thrift stores, and lots of closeout items purchased from Wal-Mart, Target, Big Lots, Best Buy, and other local merchants.

My favorite place to buy stuff though is on eBay. People give away so many things every day, because they don't know what they have, or they don't have the vision to add value to the items they have. Other people just won't spend the time to build value into the items they sell by writing a full description and adding good pictures. I'll bet I could make at least a thousand dollars a month, probably a whole lot more, just buying poorly listed items and repackaging them.

Before you go

Thank you for reading this book. If you enjoyed it, or found it helpful, I'd be grateful if you'd post a short review. Your review really does help. It helps other readers decide if this book would be a good investment for them, and it helps me to make this an even better book for you. I personally read all of the reviews my books receive, and based on what readers tell me, I can make my books even better, and include the kind of information readers want and need.

Thanks again for choosing my book, and here's wishing you great success in your online selling.

Amazon page: amazon.com/author/nickvulich

Blog: http://www.indieauthorstoolbox.com/

Email: hi@nickvulich.com

Bonus excerpt

(This is an excerpt from my most recent book – **Indie Author's Toolbox.** *If you've ever wanted to self-publish your own book,* Indie Author's Toolbox *is the ultimate reference. You will learn how to select a hot subject, how to optimize your book on and off of Amazon, and how to market your book so you can get the power of Amazon behind you – helping to promote your book.)*

Optimize your book on Amazon

Psst! Do you wanna know a secret?

There are no secrets. No tricks. No magical incantations you can invoke to sell more books on Amazon, or any other online book site for that matter.

Selling more books is all about how you manage the basics.

It's about -

1) Writing a good book

2) Selecting a killer title

3) Creating an attention grabbing cover

4) Writing a book description that compels readers to click the buy button

5) Choosing keywords that drive searchers to your book

6) Ensuring your "look inside" sample sells your book

If you can do these six steps well your book is going to sell. Misfire on any of them, and you're going to have problems.

Just so you know some of the advice I'm going to give you here goes contrary to what you're going to get from most of the "experts." In my two years of indie publishing, I've taken a lot of wrong turns. I've been fed a lot of bad advice. All I can tell you is what has worked best for me. Best advice I can give you is to experiment often. Don't be afraid to try new things. Keep the ones that work, discard the ones that don't. Keep building your bag of tricks, and over time you'll develop a system that'll work for you.

With that said, let's dig deeper into each step and see how you can use them to position your book for success.

Write a good book. Abraham Lincoln said it best, "You can fool all the people some of the time, and some of the people all the time, but you cannot fool all the people all the time."

If you don't have a good book, the reviews are going to catch up to you, and people are going to stop buying your book. Sure. You can sell a few copies of a bad book. Sometimes you can sell a whole lot of copies, but eventually the reviews are going to kill your career.

There are a lot of Kindle advice writers telling aspiring authors you don't have to write well. Don't waste too much time editing your work. Just do the best you can, and get your book out there. Sell a few copies, and then write your next book.

Last year, or the year before, that advice might have worked. But readers are getting smarter. They've downloaded a lot of worthless crap over the past few years, and they're tired of it. If you don't believe me, read the reviews. Most readers are honest, and they call it like they see it. If you're book smells like a load of horse hockey, they're going to say it. If enough readers jump on the band wagon, there's no going back.

Forget the books that tell you how to write a book before breakfast, over your lunch break, or on a roll of toilet paper while you're sitting on the throne. At the same time, forget the books that tell you you can write a book in seven days, twenty-one days, or even thirty days. The fact is you can write a book in the time it takes you, no sooner, and no later.

There appears to be a fundamental disconnect between what readers want, and what some writers think readers want. Many writers believe readers want to read short books. The majority of reviewers say just the opposite – here are a few of the reviews major novelists recently received for their Kindle Shorts.

. *A throw away sixty pages.* **Lee Child**

. *Don't waste time and money buying the ads, wait for the book itself.* **Janet Evanovich**

. *It's so short it isn't even a short story.* **Dean Koontz.**

. *Good writing for the beginning of a novel, with no real ending.* **Steven King**

No matter what anyone tells you, most readers don't like short. It makes them feel like they missed out on something, or that the writer was just out to take their money. Consider this the next time you go to publish a short manuscript.

The key to selling more books is to write a complete book that leaves readers satisfied. If you can do this, you're golden. You will get enthusiastic reviews. Readers will tell their friends about you. They will race out to buy your books the first day they're released.

Select a killer title. Too many writers try to stuff a load of keywords into their title hoping they can game the system. Search engines may find keyword bloated titles enticing, but real readers are turned off by titles too big to fit on the book cover. They can't remember them. They don't understand them. They don't know what to think about books that use them.

Short is better.

One to three words is the perfect length for a title. It's easy to remember. There's very little chance for confusion. As a result, you're going to sell more books.

Check out the following five titles. They're short. They're memorable. They do a good job of revealing what the book is about. And, if I didn't mention it, they're selling a lot of books.

. *Story Selling* by Nick Nanton & J. W. Dicks

. *eBay Seller Secrets* by Ann Eckhart

. *Declutter your Inbox* by S. J. Scott

. *Killing Jesus* by Bill O'Reilly

. *Email Marketing* Blueprint by Steve Scott

Compare that to these titles.

. *7 Steps to Sales Scripts for B2B Appointment Setting* by Scott Channell

. *How I Make Money Every Day Automatically When Others Sell on eBay* by Xavier Zimms

. *Author's Quick Guide to Making Money with your 99¢ Kindle Books* by Kristen Eckstein

. *How to Write and Publish your Book on Amazon and on Kindle* by Eldes Saullo

. *How to Write a Kindle Book that People Want to Buy before Breakfast* by James Bedford

Use your main keyword in your title. Use a combination of two or three keywords. Don't string together a series of two or three keyword phrases in your title. It doesn't make sense.

Instead, write a short title. Follow it up with an awesome subtitle that tells readers a little more about the subject matter of your book. Once again, keep the subtitle short. Less than ten words are best. Include your most relevant keywords in your title and subtitle. Place your other search terms where they belong – in your book tags, and in your description.

Make your cover sizzle. Readers are going to be attracted your book by three things – the title, the cover, and the buz surrounding it.

Whatever you do, don't design your cover yourself. No matter how good you think you are, or how great you think your idea is, don't design your own cover. Don't let your best friend, or baby sister do it either. Your cover is too important to be left to chance.

I gotta admit I'm a serial Fiverr. I've outsourced 179 graphic design gigs on Fiverr in the last six months. Some of the work you receive is so-so, but a lot of the gigs posted on Fiverr deliver professional quality designs. The results, like anything else, depend upon the effort you put into it.

I use **rroxx** for most of my covers. He does great work, and my projects are always delivered on time. Here's the link to his gig if you want to check it out http://www.fiverr.com/rroxx/create-awesome-professional-ebook-cover-design.

You can also outsource your cover on Elance, 99 Designs, or odesk. Each of these sites has experienced graphic designers who can help you design a professional cover to help sell your book.

The key to getting a great deign is to know what you want before you select a designer. Look at other books in your genre. You don't want to steal anyone else's design, but normally there's a common theme running through many of the book covers. If you find something you like, download that cover so you can send it to your designer. Tell them you like this cover, but you have a few ideas to change it up for your own. You can also send your designer three or four covers that you like to let them know this is the style you're thinking of.

Sometimes I know exactly what I want, and I'll put together a short sketch. Other times, I'll let the designer know I have no idea what I want. When this is the case, I normally have four or five designers create a concept for me. If none of the designs that come back are exactly what I'm looking for I'll try again. Sometimes I might like different portions of several covers, and I'll have one of the designers put it all together for me.

Most recently, I've been more concerned about controlling the images used on my book covers. Some designers on Fiverr have an upcharge to purchase clipart for you, but you never know. If they grab a piece of art without the proper license, it's your butt that's on the line for a lawsuit. Another issue I've run into is I don't remember which designer I used to make some of my earlier covers. This creates problems when I release audio books and paperbacks, because I don't know where to purchase clipart rights for the newer versions of those covers.

Because of this I've begun sourcing most of the clipart for my covers myself before giving the project to a designer. This way I know I'm legal and hold the proper licenses for all of the art work used on my covers. I get most of my clipart from Can Stock Photo, http://www.canstockphoto.com/. Their prices are reasonable and range from $2.50 to $10.00 per use.

I don't claim to be a lawyer or anything, but keep in mind, you need to pay each time you use a piece of clipart. So if your book is available as an eBook, paperback, and audio book, you need to purchase the rights to the clipart three separate times.

After I've picked out the images to use, I put together specific instructions for the cover designer.

I would like a book cover for an Audible audio book. The cover size is 2500 x 2500 pixels. It needs to be a perfect square, and all of the text and images need to be fitted to it. You cannot stretch out the original book cover to fit the space. They will reject the cover.

I am enclosing the original clipart, and a copy of the original book cover. Please keep as close to the original design as possible.

Be sure to specify the exact cover size. Even when you're ordering an eBook cover, every designer seems to deliver it in slightly different dimensions. When you order a Create Space cover, make sure you let the designer know it needs to be delivered as a .pdf file, and that it needs to conform to the Create Space sizing guidelines. I've had several designers deliver the paperback cover as a jpeg, and as a result it was unusable.

If you're ordering a paperback cover for Create Space you need to specify the trim size (example: 6 x 9), the paper style (cream or white), the page style (black and white or color), and how many pages are in your book. Your designer requires all of this information to properly size your cover. You will also need to supply any text or illustrations for the back cover blurb. If you want printing on the spine you need to specify the text.

FYI: Your book needs to be at least 120 pages to have room for a printed message on the spine.

If you're not sure about your cover or your book concept, it can be a good idea to have several covers ready to go.

That way if your book gets off to a slow start you can switch covers and see which one does a better job.

Write a compelling book description. Congratulations. You've done it. You've written an awesome title. You created a dazzling book cover. Now you've just got to close the deal.

How do you turn browsers into buyers?

A compelling book description can get readers drooling for more.

There's no right or wrong way to write a book description.

Some authors start off by asking a question. Others present a dilemma either their reader or their main character may find themselves in. Still others summarize their story. Any of these approaches can work.

What you want to do is draw readers in. Get them hooked on your story, or in the case of nonfiction, on the solution you're presenting. Make it interesting. Create suspense. Make sure they want to read more.

How do you do that?

Ask questions.

Have you ever wondered what life would be like if you took the other road? The one your parents, teachers, and friends told you would put you on a collision course with the others? What if you veered just a little off course, for just a few minutes? Would it change your destiny forever?

Make your case as an authority figure.

Fifteen years as an eBay Power Seller and Top Rated Seller gives Nick a unique combination of experience and knowledge to guide new and experienced sellers through the maze we call eBay.

Introduce your main character.

Max Power stood at the crossroads of now and forever. If he followed her into the time portal everything behind him would disappear forever. If he took the leap his future was uncertain. All Max knew for sure was the girl had saved his life back on Zeta 9. Now she was offering him a future as uncertain as the Zonderan Divide.

Compare your writing to a famous author.

Reviewers say my writing is a cross between Stephen King and Peter Straub with a touch of Kurt Vonnegut thrown in for comedy relief. Read Death Race 3000, and find out for yourself why the Zombie Jesus challenged the Werewolf Devil. Laugh your ass off. Puke your guts out. Run the full gamut of your emotions. You may never want to read another book again – Ever

Books by Nick Vulich

eBay 2014: Why You're Not Selling Anything on eBay, and What you Can Do About it

Freaking Idiots Guide to Selling on eBay: How Anyone Can Make $100 or More Everyday Selling on eBay

Sell it Online: How to Make Money Selling on eBay, Amazon, Fiverr, & Etsy

How to Make Money Selling Old Books & Magazines on eBay

eBay Subject Matter Expert: 5 Weeks to becoming an eBay Subject Matter Expert

Indie Authors Toolbox

Audio Books by Nick Vulich

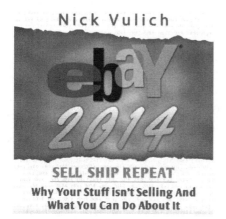

eBay 2014: Why Your Stuff Isn't Selling And What You Can Do About It

Freaking Idiots guide to Selling on eBay: How anyone can make $100 or more everyday selling on eBay

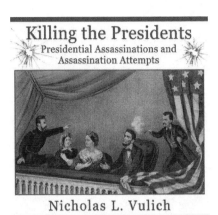

Killing the Presidents
Presidential Assassinations and Assassination Attempts

Nicholas L. Vulich

Killing the Presidents: Presidential Assassinations and Assassination Attempts

Manage Like Abraham Lincoln

Made in the USA
Middletown, DE
12 November 2015